PRAISE FOR
THE POWER OF SOLITUDE

In this amazing book, born out of rich experience, deep insight, and strong Christian commitment, Annemarie Kidder explores the promise and power of solitude in both its ancient and contemporary settings, revealing it as a physical and spiritual quest born out of our deepest longing for connections. Drawing on psychological, theological, mystical, and poetic writers, she skillfully interweaves themes of contemporary life with the ancient wisdom of Christian spirituality. Her reflections illuminate the landscape of the soul, the search for wholeness of body, mind, and spirit, the tension between union and separateness, connection and communion, in ourselves and others. This book is full of wise counsel and expert guidance on the path to a deeper knowledge of God.

—URSULA KING, professor of theology and
religious studies, University of Bristol, England

The Power of Solitude is the work of an impressive scholar who has the unique ability of weaving her own experience with that of her readers to pursue the challenge and rewards of solitude in the everydayness of life. At the same time she explores its roots within the biblical, patristic, and monastic traditions while engaging contemporary insights of novelists, poets, pastors, psychologists, and theologians. This is both a rare accomplishment and an intriguing one— inspiring, nourishing, and instructing at the same time.

—MARGARET BRENNAN, I.H.M., professor emerita,
Regis College, Toronto

Dr. Annemarie Kidder has written an excellent, finely reasoned book on the subject of solitude, presented with skill and artistry. Dr. Kidder's approach is based on solid scholarship in the field. She has gathered insight from a wide range of religious thinkers and traditions, including poets, to elucidate this subject that is so timely in its approach to our modern dilemma of searching for meaning in the Christian community and in life generally. The book delves into the historical precedents of religious communities, going back to the earliest Christian traditions, and even before that to the foremost prophets and their solid and solitary relationship with God, to the early church fathers who founded monastic communities, to the thinkers who have written about their own contemplative experiences of prayer and solitude. A nice touch is that she includes some personal religious experiences, which add depth and dimension to the more formal discussion. The early childhood services in her hometown in Germany come to life beautifully, sensually, and visually in the discussion on mysticism. She sums up the experience in almost mystical terms, "God ... concealed and revealed, silent and vocal, elusive and in plain view." Dr. Kidder offers a close and nuanced study of solitude in an engaging, readable form that entices the reader to the end.

—ASTRID B. BECK, managing editor,
the Anchor Bible Dictionary and
the Eerdmans Bible Dictionary

The Power of
Solitude

The Power of Solitude

*Discovering Your True Self
in a World of Nonsense and Noise*

Annemarie S. Kidder

Foreword by
Eugene H. Peterson

A Crossroad Book
The Crossroad Publishing Company
New York

The Crossroad Publishing Company
16 Penn Plaza–481 Eighth Avenue, Suite 1550
New York, NY 10001

Printed in the United States of America

The text of this book is set in 11/14 Stone Informal.
The display face is Calligraphic 421.

Library of Congress Cataloging-in-Publication Data

Kidder, Annemarie S.
   The Power of solitude : discovering your true self in a world
of nonsense and noise / Annemarie S. Kidder ; foreword by
Eugene H. Peterson.
      p. cm.
   Includes bibliographical references.
   ISBN-13: 978-0-8245-2444-9 (alk. paper)
   ISBN-10: 0-8245-2444-6 (alk. paper)
   1. Solitude–Religious aspects–Christianity. 2. Spiritual life–
Christianity. I. Title.
BV4509.5.K45 2006
248.4′7–dc22

                                        2006024397

1   2   3   4   5   6   7   8   9   10   12   11   10   09   08   07

Contents

Three
THE PRACTICES OF SOLITUDE

Foreword

Solitude in America? In *Christian* America? Hardly. We thrive on numbers and noise.

But maybe not. There is more around here than meets the eye. Or the ear. Solitude is a chosen way of life for a surprising number of men and women in this multitudinous and cacophonous country. Solitude as a deliberately cultivated discipline that provides insights and energies indispensable to living a robust Christian life. And it just so happens that these solitude-embracing lives have a surprising and creative influence on communities all over this land. Like leaven. Like salt.

When I was an adolescent, an attraction to Elijah the Tishbite gave me my first taste of the spirituality of solitude. I think it may have been because he came from the hills and mountains, was at home in a wilderness similar to the Montana Rockies I grew up in. I imagined him formed in Gilead, occasionally coming out in public to expose the idolatries and compromises of the country and give witness to the word and presence of God. I liked his boldness on Mt. Carmel, taking on the priests of Baal and calling down fire from the skies that incinerated the altar and its offering. I liked the matching drama of the final whirlwind rapture in the chariot and horses of fire. Elijah and fire.

But it took me awhile to realize that it was solitude and silence that fueled that fire. As I entered the adult world, I found myself immersed in a sea of clamoring needs and pressures that threatened to obscure or even erase my baptismal identity as Christian. Virtually everyone I met presented me with an agenda. The items on the list were usually well-intentioned and socially approved but more often than not they also involved employing an idol that could be used in substitute for the God and father of our Lord Jesus Christ in a culture dominated by consumer idolatries. How could I maintain my Christian identity? I thought one way was by keeping prayerful company with Elijah. In his company I was gradually introduced to the prevalence and power of solitude in his surprisingly (to me) vast progeny through the centuries.

In the company of Elijah I realized that the public drama at Carmel with the priests of Baal and the confrontations with Ahab and Jezebel and Ahaziah were occasional. Elijah was "a figure of absolutely primeval force" (von Rad), but the gathering and maturing of that force took place in solitude along the margins — at the Brook Cherith hiding out with the ravens, in obscurity with the widow of Zaraphath in Sidon, in despair under the broom tree in the wilderness of Beersheba, trudging for forty days and nights across desert wastes and ending up alone in an isolated cave on the bare granite face of Sinai. It was there that Elijah recovered his, by that time severely battered, prophetic vocation. But not by means of fire from the heavens, rather in solitude and silence, in God's gentle, quiet whisper, "sheer silence." The Hebrew phrase is tantalizingly elusive. St. John of the Cross, one of our most notable solitaries, gets it right: "silent music...sounding solitude."

Elijah lived his life mostly in solitude, marginal to the popular religion of the day, marginal to the power politics of the day. It was from the solitary margins that Elijah re-centered the life of Israel. For people schooled in a biblical imagination, the fascination with numbers and goals as a sign of efficacy and as a demonstration of God's blessing is strange indeed. Virtually all the men and women who prepared the way of the Lord, which became the way of Jesus, worked at the margins of their societies and cultures. Elijah is conspicuous but in no way unique. The story of Elijah is told from nine site locations. Only one, Mt. Carmel, provided a public stage for a crowd of people. All the others were out-of-the-way and marginal.

This is important. Elijah appeared from time to time without fanfare and then disappeared from public life without notice. Basically, he lived a solitary life in obscurity. His formative impact on how we as a people of God understand responsibility and witness in society is inescapable and irreversible. It never goes out of style and by God's grace is replicated in every generation. The essence of the way of solitude is that it counters the world's way, the culture's way. We need continuous help in staying alert and knowledgeable regarding the conditions in which we cultivate faithful and obedient lives before God. For the ways of the prevailing culture, whether American, Chinese, Polish, Indonesian — its assumptions, its values, its methods of going about its work—are seldom on the side of God.

What Elijah did, and what his contemporary progeny does, is purge our imaginations of this world's assumptions on how life is lived, on what counts in life, on where the power comes from. Over and over again, God the Holy Spirit uses those who embrace solitude to separate his people from the lies and illusions they have become accustomed to and puts us back on the path of simple faith and obedience and worship of the God and Father of our Lord Jesus Christ, in defiance of all that the world admires and rewards. This company is now centuries deep and world-wide, training us, if we will let it, in the centering and energizing "power of solitude" —and discerning the difference between the ways of the world and the ways of Jesus, keeping us present to the Presence of God.

This is Annemarie Kidder's subject: solitude and the men and women who embrace it. She shows how it has worked through the centuries and how it is working now among our contemporaries. And she invites us in as participants. She immerses us by personal witness and clarifying documentation in the subterranean energy sources of solitude and silence, these huge aquifers of the Spirit, that make it possible to live robust and Christ-centered lives in this hurrying, chattering, distracted wasteland of ours.

We need this writer. We need this book.

Eugene H. Peterson
Professor Emeritus of Spiritual Theology
Regent College, Vancouver, B.C.

One

What Is the Discipline of Solitude?

Longing for Eyes

Certainty is only reserved for the wise,
those longing for eyes.[1]

I discovered this poem by Rainer Maria Rilke when I was working on a translation of his *Book of Hours*. It struck me that "longing for eyes" is precisely what motivates me to embrace the spiritual discipline of solitude. I believe that is true for others as well, even if they don't use precisely those words. We long for eyes to see ourselves, others, and our God more clearly; to see through artifice to authenticity; to see a new creation beyond the brokenness we experience each day in ourselves and the world around us. Certainty, Rilke seems to say, comes to the wise ones who continually long to see.

In the wise one we know as Jesus, we see both the richness and the rigors of the spiritual discipline of solitude. Physically, emotionally, and spiritually exhausted by the crowds that pursued him wherever he went, Jesus regularly sought out a time and place apart. In communion with God in solitude from his demanding everyday life, he refreshed his body and spirit so he could continue his work with those seekers of healing and hope who crowded around him. The richness of this solitude provided both a deep spiritual rest and the physical and emotional renewal necessary to live with both deep compassion and conviction. Solitude helped Jesus to see—and to live fully.

Yet truly seeing is not for the faint of heart, as the life of Jesus also teaches us.

In his desert solitude, before beginning his ministry, Jesus struggled with the deeply alluring temptations to power, popularity, and relevance. In the lonely, aching solitude of Gethsemane, he surrendered to the ultimate call and claim of God upon his life. And in the final, agonizing solitude of the cross, feeling abandoned even by God, he managed to commend his spirit to the Holy One.

As Jesus did, we receive solace, refreshment, and revitalization in solitude. And like Jesus, in solitude we too face temptation, terror, and abandonment. We are challenged to die in order that we might truly live. His example guides us as we seek to follow his way.

Just as we look to Jesus for guidance concerning the spiritual discipline of solitude, we can also look to his disciples. In their journey with Jesus, the disciples were repeatedly asked to let go of all that constituted their lives—their work, their families, their self-identities. At one point Peter, wondering what they had to show in exchange for their letting go — a question that we ourselves may sometimes ask — complained to Jesus, "Look, we have left everything and followed you" (Mark 10:28). In response, Jesus explains that while the rewards and benefits may be as yet invisible, they are already present. For "truly I tell you, there is no one who has left house or brothers or sisters or mother or father or children or fields, for my sake and for the sake of the good news, who will not receive a hundredfold now in this age — houses, brothers and sisters, mothers and children, and fields with persecution" (Mark 10:29–30).

This and the parallel Gospel passages suggest that the first disciples lived their "longing for eyes" as they sought to follow the one they knew as Christ. They physically removed themselves from their homes, if not permanently, then at least for some time; they distanced themselves from familial and blood ties, the bond with and obligations to mother, father, sister, brother, and children, in exchange for the "familial" bond created in the Spirit and among those who did the will of God; and they relinquished an identity defined by property. One can imagine the pain and discomfort the disciples experienced in this process of dying to self, the dilemma of having to constantly examine and redefine what was important in God's realm, the repeated failures, and the slow process of seeing a new creation take shape in them and in one another. We face the same challenges in our own journey of faith.

For the disciples, the process of seeing and bringing into being a new creation involved an ongoing practice, a deep inner listening and acute awareness of self and God, and an attempt to live, despite the crowded surroundings and communal ties, in an ongoing process of self-examination, an exchange with God that took place in solitude. They were no longer fishermen or carpenters or tax officials; they were listeners, practitioners, and activists carrying a message that could liberate people from the temporary order of life to abundant life in Christ.

How do we contemporary followers of the Way, like Jesus and his disciples, long for eyes? How do we enter into a deep inner listening and an acute awareness of ourselves and God so that we may be set free in Christ? We do this by embracing and entering into solitude with longing eyes and open hearts. When we do this, we may find ourselves experiencing something similar to what the disciples experienced: giving up much that we want to cling to, wondering who we are in our relationship with God, and dying to our old self without knowing what our new self will be.

Though there are many things we don't know, we do know that this new self cannot emerge apart from reflection and ongoing wrestling in the quiet of our own minds and hearts, in prayer, in solitude. When we do this, we must contend with our anger, resentment, anxiety, and repeated attempts of clinging to that which is not of God. If we journey honestly and courageously with Jesus, we find that, one after another, the "rugs" of our identity based on pride, power, accomplishments, and connections are pulled out from under us. And what remains? Our solitary encounter with God.

The spiritual discipline of solitude is a practice that helps our souls connect with God. It invites us to sit in the loving presence of God and to be transformed from old to new, from death to life. It also invites us to sit long enough with the pain and discomfort that arises from our all-too-human (sinful) condition so we can locate the cause of that pain, identify the attachments we cherish, and acknowledge our refusal and resistance to letting go. In this way, the spiritual discipline of solitude, when practiced consistently, educates and nourishes our souls to grow into an increased awareness and experience of God's constant presence, the fruits of which are inner happiness and peace.

2

I Need My Space

At a recent gathering that celebrated a couple's fiftieth wedding anniversary, I asked them what the secret of their long and happy marriage was. Both, as if in unison, named the other's willingness to allow for space. Each was free to pursue hobbies and avocations without being scolded and shamed. Each had a common set of friends, as well as a distinct list of personal friends. They shared a bedroom but inhabited different corners and rooms in the house. They had a common library as well as individual nooks of books and magazine racks. Without being fully aware of these arrangements, they had created a space for solitude, for sitting and checking in with their souls in slots of their own design.

The need for alone space does not dissolve in an intimate relationship, but is of crucial importance for the relationship to work. Rainer Maria Rilke addresses the issue of solitude in marriage. "The point of marriage," he says, "is not to create a quick commonality by tearing down all boundaries; on the contrary, a good marriage is one in which each partner appoints the other to be the guardian of his solitude."[1] During the initial romantic phase, this solitude may be temporarily surrendered, displaced, or ignored. Both partners say they want to spend as much time together as possible. But after some time, each person will have to identify and nurture what is uniquely his or her own to pursue and tend to, which includes the soul.

In recent years, ministers have placed greater emphasis on the place of solitude in marriage. At weddings, for example, the couple is reminded of the need for space in the symbolic ritual of the lighting of the unity candle. Three candles are placed on the communion table, two smaller ones on the outside and a bigger one in the middle. During the ritual, both of the smaller candles are lit by the mothers, representing the giving of birth. Then each partner takes his or her "birth" candle and lights the center or unity candle with it. Instead of extinguishing the "birth" candles, they put them back in place, so that three candles remain lit: the larger one representative of the new union in Christ, the two others indicative of each person's unique identity — which ideally the marriage will not snuff out, smother, or dim.

The cultivation of solitude is a process of individuation and self-definition, of becoming more fully one's self. Psychologist John Landgraf calls this cultivation process "singling" or reaching for singlehood.[2] Regardless of one's station in life or marital status, the soul is invited to work through the internal process of initial connectedness toward singlehood. Landgraf defines singlehood as "a state of existence, a way of being," and "a condition of encouraging, affirming, and maintaining one's integrity as a self," which means being willing, and learning how, to become "increasingly self-aware, self-preserving, self-affirming, self-fulfilling, and autonomous."[3] One assumes responsibility for one's decisions and one's well-being. Landgraf goes as far as to say that good marriages can be made and sustained only by singles, people who are on the journey to singlehood. Instead of regarding their partner as the primary source of fulfillment and giving away power to the other, people who are fully single are able to keep their power intact while freely allowing others to keep theirs. They have what Landgraf calls "self-power awareness."[4] By embracing their autonomy, they are able to function interdependently without giving in to the fixations and dependencies that limit one's ability to be loving and free.

Regardless of marital status or involvement in an intimate relationship, one needs to hone one's integrity as a self. After all, according to Rilke, "a merging of two people is an impossibility, and where it seems to exist, it is a hemming-in, a mutual consent that robs one party or both parties of their fullest freedom and development."[5] By identifying one's integrity as a self and by treasuring it, one can treasure and honor the integrity of another, thus creating the building blocks for healthy relationship. By creating the external space of solitude, of being apart and separate at times, as well as by building up one's inner self and autonomous soul in the context of relationship, one is laying the foundation for true mutuality.

My dictionary defines solitude as "the state of being alone or remote from others."[6] It is a separateness and remoteness that can be created both physically and internally—while in a crowd or alone. Creating such remoteness or aloneness as a source of inner strength and contentment is a learning process, not as a way of avoiding social contact, but as a practice to tend to our soul's voice. In solitude, we can hear the sounds in our heads and feel the pain of what is disjointed and clamors for attention. In solitude, we can choose to listen or to speak to God without interruption. In solitude, we detect what we love and fear, what draws us and what drives us, what we regret and what we look forward to. Solitude can become a path to the holy, a way of life that puts into perspective the din and tape recordings of our schedules, our shoulds and musts, our cravings and our fears.

Seeking out and cultivating solitude is a discipline for the benefit of our soul. It may be no more difficult than the discipline of regular worship attendance, of volunteering our time, of offering our tithes. But it is certainly as important as the other disciplines, for it shapes our perceptions, our priorities, the internal at-oneness we sense with ourselves and the world. Pursuing solitude, like the other disciplines, may cause discomfort, largely because it runs counter to the dictates of Western culture. Mass production and mass consumption can flourish only in a society that places value on having what the other has, having more of it, and ultimately fitting in. Bent on selling goods to the greatest number of people, the consumerist mentality objects to the individual and autonomous self and hence views with suspicion the state of being alone and separate.

An example of Western culture's distaste of solitude is the daily media barrage that exhorts us to stay connected, to keep in touch, and to communicate more efficiently. The means to that end are presented as indispensable lifelines to a better, more fulfilled existence. High-speed Internet access, cellular phones, Federal Express service, pagers, accounts that hold ever larger file sizes, cable television, satellite dishes — all of them promise to connect us with one another and with world affairs, thus generating the illusion that at any moment we are "in touch" or able to reach out and touch someone. With electronic devices at our fingertips, the measure of connectedness is defined by transmission speed, the clarity of reception, and response time. We can be reached easily, regardless of whether we are taking a shower or sitting in an airplane on the tarmac. And we can reach others with the same ease, accessing e-mail accounts and pushing the speed-dial on our cellular phone. As convenient as these technological advances are, they also keep us sedated and safely ensconced in the illusion that we are in tune and in touch with the pulsing flow of life. Moreover, they distract us from connecting with the central "computer" that is registering and storing messages for us, namely, ourselves. And the more we make ourselves technologically available to be reached and to reach out, the more we are interrupted in the effort to connect with our soul.

In my own case, the availability of communications equipment acts like a drug. When I am on vacation in a rustic country setting, for example, all I can think of is the numerous e-mails that might be piling up in my absence.

I miss hitting the "connect" key and the magic of the little electronic voice announcing that I have mail. I miss squeezing into a few spare minutes the thrill of the feeling that someone thought of me, that someone answered an e-mail I had sent, that I am remembered and included in their thoughts (or at least on their e-mail list). Even on my day off, when I am practicing e-mail abstinence, I can't help toying with the program button that would launch me into cyberspace. Other than leaving the house, not much else seems to help, and the temptation, especially when I am working at my computer, is usually greater than my good intentions. By midafternoon I am exhausted from the effort it took to resist, and, sad to say, I give in. I can't help it. I need to be connected. And I have to be reassured that since I last checked in someone has remembered to connect with me.

Electronic tools promise to bring newsworthy bites of information that keep us up-to-date and increase the wealth of what we know. Knowledge is power, we say. And the exchange of news bites, no matter how insubstantial, suggests that we are in possession of something that might serve us well. Who knows when we might be able to let our "informedness" shine, regardless of whether we caught the news on the television set or by the water cooler at work? New information also dazzles us at the moment we receive it. There is a sense of drama and activity, our pulse beats faster, and new life seems to be circulating through our living room and the inner sanctuary of our minds. Thus stimulated and teased, the mind busies itself with the task of reintegrating the new with the old and restoring a sense of cognitive balance. The only problem is that while the mind is thus occupied, the soul is still hungry and waiting for care.

3

What Are These Words
That You Are Exchanging?

In the Gospel of Luke, we read that the preoccupation with news bites and information exchange is not unique to our time (Luke 24:13–35). Two men are exchanging tidbits of information that had just come hot off the Jerusalem press: Have you not heard? They are saying.... Would you believe? What do you make of that? They walk for seven miles speculating on what they have heard, comparing notes, and correcting each other with their version of truth. Hardly do they notice when a third man joins them for the walk. "What are these words that you are exchanging with one another as you are walking?" he finally asks (Luke 24:17 NASB). Startled and perhaps a little annoyed by the interruption, the two men stand still and look sad. They tell of the death of Jesus, whom people had hoped to be the redeemer of Israel; of the women who had gone to Jesus' tomb and found it empty; of the angels the women had reported seeing and the angels' message that he was alive; and of others following up on the report and finding the women's story held up. The entire talk revolved around Jesus, describing his mighty words and deeds, the chief priests' and rulers' plot to kill him, and the latest happenings regarding his death and the disappearance of his body, accompanied by the appearance of angelic beings near the tomb. They were carrying on and on, while Jesus had just joined them in the person of the stranger whom they do not recognize. Exchanging pieces of information from reliable sources and eyewitnesses, they are incapable of becoming eyewitnesses themselves. And intent on communicating the details of what they know, they fail to commune, to be with, the one whose company they share.

We are surprised that the two men fail to recognize Jesus even when he starts talking. In a lecture on prophetic predictions concerning himself, Jesus takes them back to Moses and reminds them of the prophets' voices through the ages. Still they remain blind and deaf. We might say they are in communications-exchange mode, instead of communing mode. Absorbed in the past, they fail to recognize the one before them in the present. And they focus on *doing* and urging the stranger to stay for dinner and preparing dinner, rather than simply *being* and *seeing.* Only when the three sit down to eat and the stranger is invited to break the first loaf of bread as a gesture of hospitality do the two men begin communing. As they receive the bread Jesus has broken for them, they partake not of information but of presence, the presence of the one who is among them. And "their eyes were opened, and they recognized him" (v. 31).

Neither the two men's words nor those of Jesus create communion. Communion comes with a gesture. Bodies are poised, arms extended, eyes interlocked. Communing is more than the exchange of words and processing the incoming information. It involves one's whole being—mind, body, and soul—and a self-forgetfulness that opens us up to the present moment and invites us to simply be.

We wish that the moment of communion were prolonged and that we could read a detailed account of the experience. But Luke reports that when the two men's eyes were opened, Jesus immediately "vanished from their sight" (v. 31). Left alone again, the two disciples look back on their journey together. "Were not our hearts burning within us while he was talking to us on the road," they ask, "while he was opening the scriptures to us?" (v. 32). Had they not felt something distinctly moving and hopeful? They wanted to connect with this stranger, true, but they went about it with their heads. And because they could not move from the head to the heart, from the mind to the soul, they did not commune with the one whose death they mourned.

Like those men on the road to Emmaus, to cope with the pain of loss and loneliness we often become overly active and talkative. We read books on pain and symptoms of grief, we talk to friends about our distress, and we think that the right description of what ails us and an understanding of what promises relief will bring us healing. All the while, the divine presence stands by, waiting to be invited into our midst. In our frenzy to create connectedness, we miss out on connecting with what and whom is within reach, namely, the divine presence within the soul.

Connecting with our soul means to take note of our painful emotions and to sit with them without resorting to distracting activity. Unfortunately our soul often works slowly while our minds rush ahead and look for immediate explanations for everything. Pastor and poet Eugene H. Peterson tells the story of getting carried away like that. He had taken his nine-year-old daughter, Karen, to a nursing home to visit a woman in an advanced stage of dementia. During their visit, the woman only told one story, and she told it over and over again. Embarrassed by the incident, Peterson felt the need to explain to his daughter the woman's condition and her inability to remember properly. But the daughter was not embarrassed at all. "She wasn't trying to tell us any *thing*," the girl explained to her dad. "She was telling us who she *is*."[1] Often we miss out on understanding who someone is because we are primed to hear only what the person does. God in Christ seeks to be present with us in the presence of others. If our minds remain captivated by what others do, we may miss the presence of God flowing through them as they tell us, verbally or nonverbally, who they are.

Like the two men on the road to Emmaus who are joined by a stranger, we need to halt our activities, sit down, and see. When we stop identifying with our *doing,* we can begin *being,* and as we stop doing just for the sake of doing, we can begin communing and seeing the stranger as part of ourselves. In communing with one another, we let down our defenses and preconceived notions of reality. We receive the true presence of the other, and in doing so, we also receive the presence of Christ. Communing presupposes an act of solitude in which we allow both ourselves and others simply to be. And in that being, in that sacred solitude, we recognize Christ in others and ourselves.

4

Buoyed by and Drowned in Community

In my pastoral work, I regularly facilitate new member classes. Participants who are interested in exploring our church for membership meet on Sunday mornings for four consecutive sessions, and at our first introductory meeting they have the opportunity to share their faith journey and give the reasons they are drawn to our church. Most of them have been affiliated with another church prior to ours. Often their decision to switch churches is prompted by a sense of dissatisfaction. They say that their old church no longer fits who they are. Or they have observed or been involved in conflicts while serving in a leadership position and are burned out or discouraged. Their increased involvement and participation had brought them face to face with their denomination's and their community's shortcomings. And because their identity is closely associated with their church's community, they feel the need to exchange the community with another, a more perfect representation of who they think they are or would like to be. They think they are looking for a better "fit," when in reality they may be looking for an improved image of themselves.

Building connection, maintaining friendship, nurturing fellowship—all are considered building blocks in the emergence of a healthy self. But the popular emphasis on community and relationship has blurred the boundaries between a personality that is self-differentiated and interdependent and one that is dependent on others for self-definition. Often the participation in and belonging to a certain community covers up and overshadows the soul's need to develop an autonomous self. By over-identification with the community, the soul is drowned by external demands and unable to hear its own pulse and life. Stepping back from these external demands, taking stock of where community ends and the "I" begins will require solitude. Reflection, soul-searching, self-examination are needed for the autonomous self to emerge that is aware of veiled projections, irrational expectations, and blurred boundaries. When the need to belong overpowers our need to become and to simply be, we give greater importance to externals than internals, to public image than personal growth, to others' voices than God's voice whispering in the soul.

How then can I protect my soul from becoming drowned in community? It is, I believe, by reflecting on the benefits of community in relation to who I am and my emerging autonomous self. As someone who is single without living relatives, I am particularly sensitive to the types of community I have chosen and that have chosen me. Apart from the people I serve and work with at church, the community that I live in both mirrors and socializes my soul. For example, up until a few years ago, I lived in a garden apartment in a complex of more than a hundred units. Amid the regular flux of people moving in and moving out, there was the one constant that formed the hub of this loosely knit community: our apartment manager. Ever gregarious and outgoing, she would welcome, even solicit, our problems. If the faucet was dripping, her fingers jumped to the dial; if work gave me trouble, she lent wisdom and perspective; and if my spirits were low, she could recommend a concert or show, along with the names of several good massage therapists. But her talents did not stop there. For she had the ability to connect us with one another depending on our shared interests, needed skills, or professional expertise. A young man who treasured his solitary morning walks agreed to take me along on weekly hikes. A single mother allowed me to babysit, despite my marginal experience with infant care. An hourly laborer, who worked in a nursery by day and in a factory by night, showed me the correct way to transplant seedlings. An older couple tended to the potted plants on my patio during my vacation. A young man struggling with alcoholism proudly fed, cuddled, and entertained my cat when I was gone. A family on food stamps permitted me to take their lonely and fierce-looking bulldog for occasional walks. Our manager made it her business to see to it that we benefited from the proximity in which we lived. As a result, I discovered that some of my problems were too trivial to be dignified with ongoing attention. And as I recognized both the plight and the gifts of my neighbors, I saw my own plight diminish and my appreciation of others' gifts increase.

Two years ago I moved into a much smaller community, a condominium complex with neatly manicured and landscaped surroundings that holds annual picnics, a spring garden cleanup, and monthly board meetings. Most of us are on a first-name basis, rely on each other's watchfulness for strangers and the occasional raccoon that crawls into the attic, and offer to pet sit and water flower pots. The knowledge that someone is there to call on in case of illness or emergency gives me a sense of peace. And the prospect that any one of my neighbors might be a potential cat sitter gives me an added incentive to do my share in maintaining harmony.

A second benefit of my community is less obvious: learning patience and being willing to give up what I think is right for the good of the community. For example, our condo association subscribes to more than eighty channels of cable television, which seems excessive to someone like me, who prior to moving here did not even own a television set. There have been many times when I felt like one of the guests at the house of Simon of Bethany, bemoaning the frivolous and extravagant use of our funds, just as there have been times when I thought the expense of having new wrought-iron streetlights installed was poor stewardship. Living with the choices our board has made and publicly embracing their actions, especially since I did not bother to attend board meetings to voice my protest, invites me to practice group-mindedness and putting the well-being of the group ahead of my own. If the majority of our residents, most of them retired, favor subscribing to all these television channels; if they believe the upscale lighting fixtures will benefit us and our safety, who am I to grumble and disagree? I may not be happy with the outcome, but for the sake of the community I will hold my tongue and peace.

The educator Parker Palmer has written at length on the nature of community. In a pure community, he says, "we will not choose our companions," for they "will be given to us by grace."[1] Often they are people who will upset our settled view of self and the world. They will turn our preferences on their head, will startle us into anger and self-defense, and will take our breath away by their insistence on values that are the exact opposite of ours. True community, according to Palmer, is "that place where the person you least want to live with always lives."[2] And so, the benefit, though disguised, is that we will need to summon a degree of introspection, tolerance, and patience in order to cope. Unless we move away, our unpleasant and disruptive neighbors are the ones who will draw out in us both vices and virtues we never knew we had. Just as our enemies can be our most effective teachers, our unpleasant next-door neighbors can help us locate fixations and control issues we would not have acknowledged unless exposed in communal conflict.

An often overlooked example of pure community is the family. We did not choose Aunt Mable or Uncle Harry as our immediate relatives, but we are stuck with them. We can refuse to associate with them, we can malign them behind closed doors, but the truth is we will have to find some way to deal with their pathologies, paranoia, and put-downs. And just when we thought we had mastered our negative emotions, one of their most innocent words or gestures brings us face to face with the reality that we are still lacking inordinate amounts of forgiveness, forbearance, and grace.

Developing a healthy and autonomous self will require the discipline of stepping back temporarily and taking stock of how we view and use the community in which we live. Are we drawing a good deal of self-worth and pride from belonging to a certain community and its positive public image? Or does the community help us mirror who we are, extrapolating from and magnifying for us our shortcomings and selfish nature, while prompting us to grow in self-awareness and self-restraint for the benefit of the greater good? Engaging in and disengaging from community will move us back and forth between the spheres of the social and the solitary, between participating in communal life and withdrawing from it, between actively practicing who we are and holding still to see where we fall short.

5

Breathing in Unison

The ideal image of pure community, God's community in Christ, is described in the story of Pentecost (Acts 2:1–13). What was destroyed with the building of the tower of Babel, what was lost in God's scattering of the people by giving them various languages, is restored in one gusty rush of the Holy Spirit. Pentecost is the symbolic reversal and redemption of the misunderstandings and disharmony that have existed since the Babel incident. The story is an image of a future, God-intended harmony and an admonition to do our share in acting as a conduit of peace. This is especially true in our dealings with one another at church. When Jesus joined the disciples shortly after his death, he said twice, "Peace be with you" (John 20:19, 21). Then, after breathing on them, Jesus says, "Receive the Holy Spirit. If you forgive the sins of any, they are forgiven them; if you retain the sins of any, they are retained" (John 20:22–23). We repeat Jesus' words in our passing of the peace. Yet we often say it by nursing the old wounds inflicted on us by others. We work hard at keeping the pain alive by visiting and revisiting it with anyone willing to listen. And we hand over our joy and happiness in exchange for the strange allure of plotting revenge and bringing about the justice we desire. Why are we so drawn to relive our pain? It seems that the art of forgiveness is so hard because it might let someone off the hook who doesn't deserve to be. We "retain the sins" that others have committed against us as future ammunition and dividing walls. The only problem is, unless we let go and forgive, we are not going to find the peace that Jesus breathed on us.

I don't know a better way to practice community and forgiveness than coming to worship. Here we are, all so strangely different, and yet gathered into this one place with people we hardly know and with some for whom we hardly care. And then the liturgy starts, and, like toy soldiers, we are compelled to fall in line: first the opening hymn, then the common prayer of confession, another hymn, the Lord's Prayer, and more hymns. All of this activity takes breath — breathing in, breathing out. Some of us can't sing, but we will mouth the words, form the vowels, take a breath at about the same time, inhale and exhale, and take in the same air, the very same Spirit that was poured out at Jerusalem so long ago.

According to the tenets of earth science, our beautiful planet is wrapped in a protective shield called the atmosphere, which separates the air we breathe from the cold vacuum of outer space. Beneath this wrap is all the air that ever was. No cosmic cleaning company comes along to replace it every so often. The same ancient air keeps recirculating, so that each time we take a breath we breathe stardust left over from the big bang, air that has circulated through a brontosaurus, air that was breathed by Plato and Aristotle and Mozart and Bach.[1] Every time we fill our lungs with air we take in what was a newborn's first breath, and a person's last. It is the same air we breathe that hung above the chest of Jesus when he breathed his last, and it is the same air we breathe that he breathed upon the disciples to set them free. The sense of community comes with the breathing, the letting go of it all, where the breath of peace gets a chance to wash over us, where one breathes and prays in unison, where one sings and collectively lines up to take the body and the blood of Christ.

Perhaps the great marvel of Pentecost is that the peoples gathered at Jerusalem heard the disciples at all in this throbbing metropolis. But hear them they did, each of them comprehending the message of the Gospel not only in Hebrew and Greek, the common languages of that time and place, but in the language of the human heart. Now, as then, people yearn to hear words of forgiveness and peace. But it takes a quiet place, a place of solitude to hear. The cell phones need turning off, our e-mails need a Sabbath rest. Each time we give in to answering that call or checking that e-mail, we run the risk of missing out on hearing another voice, the voice of cosmic harmony and the universal divine soundtrack of which we are a part. But it's not all about immediate environment. Our own antennae may be pointing the wrong direction, so that we hear only what we want to hear, what makes us feel better about ourselves, what gives us an ego boost, which we then call the "voice of God."

Those of us who had to learn a foreign language for mere survival know what a difficult business that is. There really are no shortcuts. One has to take time to sit down and to listen, then mouth the words after the teacher or the tape, then memorize, then write down very slowly what you want to say. The language of God's community is like that. It's a foreign language that takes time and effort to learn. Unfortunately just when we think we finally have this God business all figured out, God sends a challenge: love this person who is unlovable and resides next door, accept this person for who she is, hand over your judgments and let me handle it. It's like a tape recording, but when we follow along and voice the vowels and make a bumbling effort at the words of acceptance and peace, Babel turns to Pentecost, and we are acting out and speaking the communal language of God in Christ.

Many times we are driven by an illusion of what true Christian community should look like, chasing after a dream and being disappointed by the realities. In his little book *Life Together*, the Lutheran pastor Dietrich Bonhoeffer offers practical advice to students and members of his small underground seminary community suffering from persecution by the Nazi regime. "God hates visionary dreaming," says Bonhoeffer, for "it makes the dreamer proud and pretentious." The person who "fashions a visionary ideal of community demands that it be realized by God, by others," by oneself.[2] When things do not go according to plan, one first accuses the other members, then God, then self. But since "God has already laid the only foundation of our fellowship, because God has bound us together in one body with other Christians in Jesus Christ," long before *we* arrived there and entered into life with them, "we enter into that common life not as demanders but as thankful recipients."[3]

Community, whether loose- or tight-knit, has the potential of drawing out our ingratitude, our unforgiving nature, our potential to manipulate, our inclination to force our preferences on others. Like a mirror, community reflects back to me the dissonance between my own will and that of the group. It issues an invitation to solitude, where I can recover the boundaries of a true self, consider whether I am just talking for talking's sake, and observe the degree to which I am buoyed or drowned by it. Community exposes vices—and virtues—I never thought possible, and it shakes me awake from the dreamlike pleasantries of an imaginary self I thought whole and well.

6

The Holy Longing for Connection

The dilemma of human existence is our desire to breathe in unison and in connectedness with others on the one hand, and the need of the soul to attain a sense of autonomy in solitude on the other. The ways to juggle the tension between union and separateness, between connecting and communing, is the province of spirituality. While psychology studies the human mind and behavior, spirituality studies that inner dimension of the person called the spirit or soul and its potential for transcendence. Today books on spirituality are everywhere. However, despite the plethora of literature on the subject, many still adhere to the misunderstanding that spirituality is for a select few, those mystically inclined, those spiritually oriented, or those drawn to piety and church. In reality, everyone has a spirituality, a set of directives that seek to balance the soul's urge to connect and the need to separate. Each of us struggles with the powerful energies that pull and push, driving us to find connectedness in the experience of union and warning us of its dangers.

At the root of our desire for connectedness lies our hunger to be reconnected with God. St. Augustine says that we are restless until our souls come to rest in God. However, we are prone to misdirecting our restlessness for divine connection into activities that are easier to obtain than the wisdom and knowledge of God, preferring the temporal to the eternal, the material to the spiritual, the human to the divine. The desire and longing for connectedness is God-given and holy, but it easily becomes unholy if used from selfish motives and for futile gain. Some of our urges to establish connection are not easily detected. For example, we are trying to connect our personal preferences with the outer environment when we push our views on others and try to make them comply. We are trying to connect our inner self with the outside world when finding our primary identity in our affiliation with a group, team, or party. We are trying to connect with the image of communal fashion for acceptance and praise when purchasing what is fashionable and "in."

The longing for connection is also part of our emotional responses and dispositions. We tend to respond to danger in rage or withdrawal, depending on the associations we make and the patterns we have established over a lifetime. We follow a course of action because "we have always done it that way." We adhere to thought patterns because they have proven to work for us. However, the desire to connect to the past, to an emotion we have learned to value, and then adhering to this pattern prevents change. It short-circuits our ability to create separateness and autonomy—a necessary condition for the well-being of our soul. These habits of seeking connection can then propel us into doing what St. Paul calls "the very thing I hate," finding "that when I want to do what is good, evil lies close at hand" (Rom. 7:15, 21). In his paraphrased version of the New Testament, *The Message,* Eugene Peterson puts Paul's observation in terms of modern speech: "What I don't understand about myself is that I decide one way, but then I act another, doing things I absolutely despise."

What then is this urge that seemingly drives us to connect, allowing us for little pause, and giving us hardly a moment to reflect on what we are about to do? The Roman Catholic priest and theologian Ronald Rolheiser calls it the "holy longing," or *eros,* a "spiritual energy" permeating our consciousness, burning "fires" pulsating in our bodies.[1] This soul energy is found not only in humans, but in nature as well. Rocks, plants, insects, and animals are just as relentlessly driven. "In everything," says Rolheiser, "from the atom to the human person, there is the blind power to unite with other things and to grow"[2] outward, reaching for that which is beyond itself.

Former cultures understood the fierce nature of the fire to connect. For the most part, they feared energy and buffered it in the form of religious or ethical taboos. Energy, they felt, needed some mediation, like electric current needs transformers to convert it into usable and nondestructive voltage. Rituals, taboos, and prohibitions were to protect people from the brute force of the energy that they experienced as running rampant in their bodies. According to Rolheiser, they surrounded this type of energy, especially sexual energy, with symbolic meaning, so as to properly channel it and prevent themselves from being derailed by its force. As outdated as some of the rituals and taboos may seem to us today, the ancients were able to associate the energy with something that was "coming from God and... ultimately directed back toward God."[3]

In postmodern times we have come to underestimate the powerful erotic and creative energy that drives us to unite in relationships and pushes us outward in our search for connectedness. In *Teaching a Stone to Talk,* a collection of meditations on nature and human meanings, Annie Dillard remarks on how we also underestimate the power of God. Comparing Christians to brainless tourists "on a packaged tour of the Absolute," she wonders whether any one of us while at worship has "the foggiest idea what sort of power we so blithely invoke." The churches are as if "children playing on the floor with their chemistry sets, mixing up a batch of TNT to kill a Sunday morning." And we wear straw hats and velvet hats to church, when "we should all be wearing crash helmets" and the "ushers should issue life preservers and signal flares."[4] Dillard suspects that we no longer believe a word about the powers that the Bible ascribes to God and that operate in us as the image of God. Rolheiser makes the same observation. Today, he says, "we are naïve about the nature of energy. We consider it friendly, as something we need not fear and as something we can manage all on our own, without the help of a God or of external rules and taboos."[5] As a result, we act like teenagers whose bodies are bursting with hormones, feeling that we are up to the task of coping with that tension without any rules or outside guidance. In reality, spiritual energy is fire, and a very hot one at that, and people who naïvely play with it get burned. Taboos about sex—for example, marital fidelity and chastity in singleness—are not first and foremost about morality and sin. They are about protecting people's souls from getting derailed and harmed by their impulse and desire to connect. Along with spiritual disciplines, they steer us toward delight instead of depression; toward freedom instead of enslavement to a short-lived and illusionary connectedness.

Discovering the right way to connect with God has not generally been part of how we have been taught to practice holiness or religious devotion. Much of religious activity is carried out in community, rather than in a solitary place. Going to church on Sundays, attending education events, giving of ourselves in volunteer service and outreach, offering our monetary and skills resources — all are public expressions by which one can seemingly gauge religious involvement and devotion. Who dares talk about one's private religious life, the practices of prayer, contemplation, scripture reading, study, sitting still? The moment we talk about solitary religious activity, it becomes partially public. Unless we balance public and private religious activities, alternating between acts that parishioners can see and those only in God's purview, we run the risk of disconnecting from God and from ourselves.

Jesus constantly reminded the religiously minded that they were exhibiting religious activity without spiritual quality. Their religious practices did not lead them into deeper communion with God. They washed the outside of their cups, while the inside remained dirty. Instead of stoking the fire toward a connection and union with God, they channeled it into buttressing their position in society. Their energy and holy longing to connect was directed at boosting their own ego and expanding their levels of influence and control. When Jesus repeatedly challenged the illusion that they were connected to God, he incited the wrath of religious groups of his time. After only a few years, they directed their energy toward eliminating and killing the one who had questioned them. Religious activity is no guarantee of God-connectedness. Even more troubling, it may be a way of avoiding the true and painful and solitary path toward communion with God, in which we must scrutinize our motives and acknowledge that we are neither connected with God nor our soul.

Much of the writing and speaking ministry of the internationally acclaimed Jesuit priest Anthony de Mello was to wake people up from their slumber of religiosity. In his book *Awareness: The Perils and Opportunities of Reality,* de Mello challenges readers to give up the masquerade of their religious activity and charity and "to tear away the tentacles of society that have enveloped and suffocated your being."[6] This is like inviting yourself to die, he says, and "only someone who has attempted this knows the terrors of the process."[7] Absorption and preoccupation with relationships or religious activity, attachments to the past or to an anticipated future, or infatuation with one's self may be signs that we are empty because we are far from God. Eventually, though, as we wait in the vast desert of solitude, we "will understand what freedom is, what love is, what happiness is, what reality is, what truth is, what God is."[8]

We are met in solitude by divine energy. When we put aside our attachments, the fire in us is allowed to flow toward and connect us with God instead of toward temporary delights. Spirituality helps us direct our internal fire toward the Holy. Religious activity, at its best, gives us time-tested venues in which to acknowledge and funnel the fire for the benefit of the religious community, the communion of saints, the company of Christ's church, the world. Unfortunately, much religious activity remains devoid of fire, lacking the ability to help us wake up and see.

In a distressing and haunting parable, de Mello illustrates what may be our own experience with religious activity and organized religion: "There was a man who invented the art of making fire. He took his tools and went to a tribe in the north, where it was very cold, bitterly cold. He taught the people there to make fire. The people were very interested. He showed them the uses to which they could put fire — they could cook, keep themselves warm, etc. They were so grateful that they had learned the art of making fire. But before they could express their gratitude to the man, he disappeared. He wasn't concerned with getting their recognition or gratitude; he was concerned about their well-being. He went to another tribe, where he again began to show them the value of his invention. People were interested there, too, a bit too interested for the peace of mind of their priests, who began to notice that this man was drawing crowds and they were losing their popularity. So they decided to do away with him. They poisoned him, crucified him, put it any way you like. But they were afraid now that the people might turn against them, so they were very wise, even wily. Do you know what they did? They had a portrait of the man made and mounted it on the main altar of the temple. The instruments for making fire were placed in front of the portrait, and the people were taught to revere the portrait and to pay reverence to the instruments of fire, which they dutifully did for centuries. The veneration and the worship went on, but there was no fire."[9]

It is tempting to assume that religious activity in general will take us to the place of God. According to de Mello, the litmus test is this: If our religious activity is not stoking the fire, if adoration and service is not kindling the flame of love, if the liturgy is not leading to "a clearer perception of reality," then our religious activity is of little use and only adds to creating "more division, more fanaticism, more antagonism."[10] By examining the fruits and end results of our religious activity, we may come to realize that we do not need more activity, but a greater respect for the fire burning in us and an increased awareness of how to direct it toward its holy source, instead.

7

Don't You Believe in Love?

In Western culture, the fire of romance has become a heavily traded commodity. Falling in love and being in love with one's partner promises happiness and bliss. Hardly a day goes by where we are not exposed to and lured by the promise of romantic love. We can't turn on the radio or TV, we can't drive down the road or highway without being made aware that "true love" might be missing from our life, that it exists, and that it can exist for us. The lyrics of popular music, the story lines of best-selling novels, the movie plots of box-office hits, along with reality shows and personality features all trade in this highly prized commodity. And we, as ever-willing consumers of a multibillion dollar entertainment industry, buy shares in hopes of receiving dividends. Like characters in a fairy tale, we identify with the story's protagonists and trust that we can one day "live happily ever after," provided we find just the right person.

Surprisingly, the idea of romance between two people is a relatively recent phenomenon in Western literary culture. According to medievalist Albrecht Classen, the notion of courtly, romantic love originated in the early twelfth century in Aquitaine, France. It was expressed in poetic literature and troubadour poetry and had as its central focus "the admiration of an aristocratic lover for a chaste and unobtainable lady."[1] Much of this type of poetry discusses the romantic aspects of love: lamenting the suffering in love's service, on the one hand, while rejoicing over the happiness it provides, on the other. While the poetry varied in genre, style, and imagery, it shared the ideal of romantic love "as a pastime for court members who, once having subscribed to love, experienced a profound change in their ideals, manners, . . . and interaction with other members of the court."[2]

The early troubadours were noblemen who entertained themselves and their courts by composing love songs. The prominent theme in the earliest body of Western romantic poetry — adding up to about 2,500 songs composed by about 460 poets — is ethical in nature. The lover's qualities are to be those of moderation, generosity, youthfulness, and joy, producing *cortesia* (courtliness), a descriptor of the knight's overall social behavior, and the origin of our word "courtesy." As the ideals of courtly and romantic love spread throughout France, producing such noted poets as Christine de Pizan, Charles d'Orléans, and François Villon, Middle High German love poetry (*Minnesang*) sprang up along the Danube and among the Hohenstaufen courts in

Germany. A key role was played by Walther von der Vo-
gelweide (ca. 1170–ca. 1230 C.E.), who began debating
with his colleagues the conflict between purely esoteric, un-
requited love and fulfilled, physical love. And the famous
"Strawberry-Song" by the Wild Alexander combined the traditional idea of falling and being in love with the biblical
theme of "the loss of innocence in Paradise" and "the bite
of a snake."[3]

By the thirteen century, the ideal of courtly love had
spread to Italy and Sicily, with the school of the *dolce stil
nuovo,* represented by Dante Alighieri and Petrarch. According to Classen, Dante Alighieri (1265–1321 C.E.) was the
first to coin the phrase *dolce stil nuovo* in his *Divina Comme-
dia* (*Purgatorio* 24.57). And the "court of the Hohenstaufen
Emperor Frederick II (1194–1250 C.E.) was the centre of
a 'Sicilian school' of poets, . . . who later deeply influenced
the rise of courtly love poetry in Tuscany and elsewhere in
northern Italy. These poets, primarily following their Occi-
tan and French forerunners, composed love songs in which
the admiration of their lady assumes religious overtones,
and where the nobility of the heart (*cor gentil*) and admiration of a godlike lady (*donna*) play a major role. Some of the
stilnovisti were deeply influenced by the new theology developed by St. Francis of Assisi (1182–1226 C.E.), emphasizing
the unity with nature in the adoration of God."[4]

By the fifteenth century, courtly love poetry was practiced all over medieval Europe, though its popularity waned
during the Enlightenment, with its emphasis on human reason. The idea of romantic love revived around 1800 C.E.
A new movement, aptly called Romanticism, rejected the
idea that human existence was defined solely by reason and
logic. The new movement praised emotion and intuition. It
emphasized the importance of the sensory world and the

subjective experience of the individual, and it reached toward the world of imagination and fantasy — a world, in short, that was rooted in an idealized past or a utopian future. This romantic idea has had a profound impact not only on art and literature but also on politics and other aspects of Western culture, and its impact continues to this day.

Today romance is not only the stuff of cinematic and popular dreams and a fast-selling consumer product; it has also become a quasi-religion and a substitute for the soul's spiritual quest. Looking for and finding the "right" person has replaced looking for and finding God. Practices and strategies to develop and nurture relationships for satisfying one's need for intimacy have replaced the practices of worship, devotion, and spiritual disciplines geared to develop intimacy with self and God. And experiencing the ecstasy of romantic attraction has become such a popular pastime that pursuing the joys of gaining wisdom and understanding of spiritual realities and forces seems an esoteric undertaking.

What are the forces that have displaced worship for the sake of personal relationship, divine communal fire for interpersonal ecstasy, and adoration with idolization? The most appealing aspect of romance may be what psychiatrist Howard Cutler calls the "ultimate ecstasy," namely, the feeling of falling in love. The ingredients of this "potent cocktail" are cultural, biological, and psychological in nature and represent the forces responsible for our drive to seek this feeling.[5] In addition to contemporary culture's romanticized notion of love, there are biological forces that have been programmed into our genes from birth as an "instinctual component of mating behavior." Based on evolutionary theory, the primary task of any organism is to survive — reproduce and assure the continued survival of the species. Therefore, it is in our species' best interest for people to fall in love as it "increases the odds that we will mate and reproduce."[6] Psychological forces also drive us to seek the feeling of falling in love. According to psychoanalyst Carl Gustav Jung (1875–1961), ancient philosophy had employed Greek mythology to explain the source of powerful forces innate to human existence. Therefore, mythology can help shed light on our common drives and the collective unconscious. In Plato's *Symposium*, for example, Socrates tells the myth of Aristophanes concerning the origin of sexual love. According to this myth, the original inhabitants of the Earth were round creatures with four hands and four feet, with their back and sides forming a circle. These self-sufficient sexless creatures repeatedly mocked the gods. To punish them, Zeus attacked them with thunderbolts and split them in half. Each creature was now two, each half longing to merge with the other half. The often unconscious drive toward romantic, passionate love can be seen as this ancient desire for reunion and fusion.

Psychologists also note that our drive to connect and re-unite is rooted in our earliest experience as infants, a primal state in which the child is completely merged with the parent or primary caregiver. According to Cutler, "evidence suggests that newborn infants do not distinguish between themselves and the rest of the universe." They do not "know where they end and the 'other' begins, lacking what is known as 'object permanence'":[7] if they are not interacting with an object, to them the object does not exist. Some part in us may still seek to regress to an earlier state of existence, a state of bliss in which there is no feeling of isolation, no feeling of separation. The merging with the lover when one is in love echoes the experience of being merged with the mother in infancy. From the perspective of object permanence in infancy, however, the feeling of being in love may also approximate the sensation of being in a godlike state, of having absolute freedom and abandon, and a sense of omnipotence. In a poem titled "First Hour," New York State poet laureate Sharon Olds highlights the potential sensations of the newborn during the first hour of life:

> That hour, I was most myself. I had shrugged
> my mother slowly off, I lay there
> taking my first breaths, as if
> the air of the room was blowing me
> like a bubble. All I had to do
> was go out along the line of my gaze and back,
> out and back, on gravity's silk, the
> pressure of the air a caress, smelling on my
> self her creamy blood....

And then comes the concluding observation about this state of short-lived postnatal innocence, the sense of autonomy and freedom and the feeling of walking on clouds — all sensations accompanying the romantic euphoria:

> I hated no one. I gazed and gazed,
> and everything was interesting, I was
> free, not yet in love, I did not
> belong to anyone, I had drunk
> no milk, yet—no one had
> my heart. I was not very human. I did not
> know there was anyone else. I lay
> like a god, for an hour.... [8]

Lovers can act like fools. There is a quality to romantic love that seems infantile and childish. People in love are said to be out of touch with reality. They are on top of the world, unfettered by physical constraints. No one matters,

neither job nor family nor friends; obligations and responsibilities recede. Even the object of one's infatuation is of
little concern, for he or she is precisely that—an object and
means needed for the euphoric state. Instead of a mutual
and mature give-and-take in relationship, it is a childish,
self-absorbed, one-sided taking it all. On the flipside of
romance one finds the element of the divine and the miraculous. Being in love feels like having the godlike attributes
of omniscience and omnipotence, being fully conscious and
aware, being all-powerful and beyond vulnerability. Is it
any wonder that we long for the euphoria of romance, for
the first hour of infancy, for a godlike state, regardless of its
fleeting and illusionary nature?

I recently met with a woman friend over lunch. She is
in her fifties, single, without children, and runs a success-
ful practice as an acupuncturist. By common standards,
she would be called physically and sexually attractive, spiritually attuned, and intellectually stimulating. When we
walk into a restaurant I notice that heads turn to look at
her. But this was not our usual lunch meeting. With bated
breath and a secretive smile, she told me that she had finally taken the plunge. What plunge? I asked, not a little
alarmed. The plunge, she said, into online dating. Of my
single women friends, at least half have their picture posted
as part of the electronic dating pool. As a result, our conversations have come to revolve around the dating scene,
the thrill and the possibility of "things getting serious" with
the special "someone I just met." But these conversations,
now that I come to think of it, have also become one-sided.
I listen mostly; they talk. I comment on the illusion and the
short-lived nature of romance, the dangers of playing with
fire, and—assuming the object of their quest is marriage—
the delimiting nature of marriage regarding matters of the
Spirit and one's freedom in Christ. I quote Paul's advice to

the Corinthians, talk about each "yes" to one thing being conversely a "no" to a host of other things, and try to gently point out the practicality and impracticality of marriage for economically secure women in midlife, based on personal experience and the observations of those who come with better credentials than I. In turn, my friends smile benevolently and act as if I had just said something completely off the subject, while waiting for their turn to speak again. They insist that romance is real, that they know countless couples who have found happiness — whether through online matching and dating services or otherwise — and that they are reasonably sure that such happiness is waiting for them as well. In addition, they argue that they are finally at a point in their life where they can "afford" it, like buying a brand new car or a house or taking a trip around the world.

Oscar Wilde said that "when one is in love, one always begins by deceiving oneself, and one always ends up by deceiving others. That is what the world calls a romance."[9] I wonder how many people who date do so out of an attraction to the realities of married life rather than the promise of romance. How many couples are romantically involved and get married basing their expectations of married life on the idealized image they had of the other when first in love? It seems there is a certain advantage and wisdom inherent in the ancient traditions of matchmaking that are still practiced today in Asia, India, and Arab countries: families of comparable social and economic standing promise one another's children at a young age to be married as early as puberty, so the fire of romantic illusion and deception has no say in the choice of the partner or in creating the impression that romance is what marriage is all about.

In his book *SoulMates*, Thomas Moore concurs that romantic love is an illusion. Most of us discover this truth at the end of a love affair when the idealized image of the

beloved has faded, the love bubble burst, or the fire of ecstasy been turned low in marriage. But he also points out
that the word "illusion" comes from the Latin *in ludere,* "to
be at play." Though an illusion, romantic love, says Moore,
"is one of the most powerful means for pulling us out of lit-
eral life and into play." Keeping the Latin in mind helps us
"remember that illusion can have a playful, even sporting
aspect."[10] For in the state of being deceived, "soul can create
something out of the stuff of our emotions and fantasies."[11]
It is an invitation to live on the edge, to balance the ordinary life with the life of the imagination, and to truly enlist
the passions of the heart. Despite the danger of becoming
fixated on an idealistic image in romantic love, this type of
fire presages and intimates the divine flame and presence
where we become as playful as infants, as light-hearted and
joyous as children of God.

The task of the soul is not to suppress our attachments to
the illusionary romantic image. Instead, we are to expose
and then release this image in surrender as an invitation
to be, to rest, to play, thus recovering the state of our child-
like, autonomous self designed for communion with God.
In his recent bestseller *The Power of Now,* Eckhart Tolle describes the romantic love relationship as an addiction that
"seems to offer liberation from a deep-seated state of fear,
need, lack, and incompleteness that is part of the human
condition."[12] But the fact that the center of one's identity
lies outside oneself, namely, in the loved one, covers up
these fears and prevents the soul from facing and processing its own pain. That is why, says Tolle, there is so much
pain in intimate relationships: "They do not cause pain
and unhappiness"; instead they *"bring out* the pain and
unhappiness that is already in you."[13] Avoidance of relationships in an attempt to avoid pain is not the answer.

Bringing the reality of the pain we bear to our attention releases and dissolves the illusion of a future happiness and helps us understand the reality of aloneness and the fact that we are close to God. Romantic love and its accompanying illusions draw us away from our center, from the soul's availability to God, from connecting with God in the here and now in a joyous and playful way. No one can fill the space reserved for God that leads to the fullness of abundant life that Jesus promised his disciples (John 10:10b). By recognizing the idolatry of romantic love that replaces devotion to God with a self-absorbed quest for happiness at the side of another person, we arrive at the place of solitude. Acknowledging our utter aloneness before God dispels the notion that a self-made happiness is within our reach. It prevents us from seeking solace outside of ourselves, from escaping God's sovereign claim on us, and from becoming our own saviors.

8

The Search for Sexual Fulfillment

The movie comedy *40 Days and 40 Nights* tells the story of a hip, twenty-something graphic designer, Matt Sullivan, who works for a dot-com company. After being dumped by his girlfriend and sleeping around to fill the void created by her absence, he has the same recurring vision: during sexual intercourse the ceiling begins to crack open and a black hole appears. Following the one-night stands and the

accompanying haunting visions, he goes to confession —
with the confessor being his own brother, a newly ordained
Roman Catholic priest. Matt has an epiphany. He resolves
to abstain from all sexual activity for the full forty days
and forty nights of Lent — in other words, no intercourse,
no masturbation, no foreplay, no viewing of pornography,
no touching or kissing of any kind. The drama and difficulties increase when our protagonist meets the woman of
his dreams shortly after taking the Lenten vow, while un-
beknownst to him his colleagues are watching his every
move with eagle eyes, betting money on the exact day he
will break his celibate vow and doing everything to make
him slip.

The movie, aimed at primarily a teen audience, was initially cross-referenced from the movie's homepage by some
Christian groups and touted as an apt tool for teaching the
benefits of sexual abstinence: getting to know the partner
on an emotional, nonphysical level first — at least for forty
days — before jumping into bed. As mixed as the reviews by
the Christian media were, underlying the plot are indeed
assumptions about the body and sexuality that have found
their way into Christian ethics and morality. First, there is
the movie trailer that reads: "One man is about to do the
unthinkable. No sex. Whatsoever. For...40 Days and 40
Nights," which is to say that men in their mid-twenties, if
not all men — and perhaps even some women — are "naturally" inclined to act out their sexual fantasies. Not doing so
borders on the supernatural (which means you need God to
help you) and approximates a superhuman and "unthinkable" feat. The body has its needs, and only an act of the
will can subdue its urges and restrain and spirit them away
on a temporary basis. Sexual activity is like any other bodily function, the movie is saying, such as eating, sleeping,
breathing, or having a bowel movement; repressing it is not

only extraordinarily hard but can lead to nervous disorders, to judge from the protagonist's recurring nightmares, fidgeting, and contorted facial expressions near the end of the forty-day fast.

Second, the movie views sexual abstinence as a hazardous undertaking, at least when practiced in isolation and on one's own accord. Nobody should subject the body to such rigorous bodily discipline for any extended and excessively long periods of time without having consulted with his or her physician first or without ongoing professional supervision. While Sullivan's young, priestly confessor could function as such a guide and physician of the soul, he does not, and, despite his role as a spokesperson of the church and member of a celibate clergy, he discourages his brother's temporary celibate practice. Thus, the church at large comes out looking like it is buying into the surrounding culture's premise that sexual activity is a natural and healthy function of the body, and sexual inactivity—even among celibate clergy—an unnatural and even potentially harmful ordeal, especially when "doing it" on your own and without the aid of a supervising mentor or community.

There is a lot of truth in the assumptions the movie makes concerning the Christian view of the body and sexual ethics, and there are a few lies as well. I shall start with the truths. If we Christians believe that the scriptures have something to say about the human body, its needs, desires, and health, what can we glean from these ancient documents concerning the body's conduct in matters of sexual activity? A brief probe into God's vision of human sexuality would begin with God's vision for human bodies, which God regards as good. But such a view does not necessarily mean that everything they *do* is good. Since with the Fall, our desires, including our sexual desires, were disordered, the task of Christian ethics is to help us to order them in the right way. The most important figure in articulating the Christian understanding of the body and sexual ethics is the Apostle Paul. In his letters to the churches, a major portion of the New Testament, he assumes that his readers value and care for their own bodies, and he understands, as they do, that bodies are the locale of longings and temptations, of desires and needs, of sexual appetites and sexual fulfillment. Paul's instructions do not recommend that we ignore or suppress these desires or needs, only that we so order them and act on them with the overall pattern of creation: with what gives life rather than death; with what gives order rather than confusion, chaos, and repression; with what fits with the larger vision of a loving and caring God who took on human form and bodily flesh in Jesus Christ and who wants our very best, rather than a God who, as an ephemeral, distant figure residing in lofty heights, desires that we suffer and come up deficient on several fronts, including the sexual.

This is the truth from a Christian perspective on sexual fulfillment. But now comes the lie—which is actually a half-truth, as are all convincing, powerful, and "good" lies — which goes like this: Since God doesn't want you to be lacking in sexual fulfillment, go for it whenever and wherever you wish, as long as you really care for that person with whom you are having sex, as long as you love that person, are committed to that person, intend to be with that person in the long run (and the list of caveats and loopholes could go on, along with other, less well-intentioned and less valiant variants that pose as excuses for sexual activity). It is a lie because, as Ignatius of Loyola would say, "The tail end of the snake is showing," with the tail end being the now unmasked desire for instant gratification of our sexual, bodily needs, whenever and wherever we want.

Paul's epistles point Christians from the whenever and wherever to the when and where, the right time and the right context of sexual activity and the gratification of our sexual needs. "I wish that all were as I myself am," he writes to the young Christians in Corinth, alluding to his own celibate practice since he was most likely a widower. But since everyone "has a particular gift from God" and not all are able to practice sexual self-control, those who are unmarried or widowed "should marry. For it is better to marry than to be aflame with passion" (1 Cor. 7:7–9). Or in the paraphrased version of *The Message,* if people "can't manage their desires and emotions, they should by all means go ahead and get married." For "the difficulties of marriage are preferable by far to a sexually tortured life as a single," and by implication, celibate, person. According to Paul then, there are only two ways in which to deal with sexual desire: one is to live with the desire without acting upon it, and the other is to obtain sexual fulfillment through intercourse with one's partner in the context of the marriage covenant. In the words of moral theologian Lewis Smedes, who summarizes Paul's thought, intercourse outside marriage is not just a minor ethical lapse, but so serious a wrong that it "must not even be mentioned among you" (Eph. 5:3). God's will is that we abstain from fornication, not giving way to the "lustful passion, like the Gentiles who do not know God" (1 Thess. 4:5). [*Porneia*] is sin; intercourse by unmarried people is [*porneia*], therefore intercourse by unmarried people is sin.[1]

In her book *Real Sex: The Naked Truth about Chastity,* Lauren Winner tells with daring honesty and evocative eloquence of her struggles as a newly baptized adult in understanding what Christians believe about and do with their sexual desires. On the one hand, she confesses, "I wanted someone to explain to me that I could be a faithful Christian and blithely continue having premarital sex" and thus "wiggle out of the church's traditional teaching." On the other, "I didn't find many of the more conservative bromides all that persuasive either — the easy proof-texting that purports to draw a coherent sexual ethic from a few verses of Paul."[2] In her quest, she has reconstructed a scriptural ethic of sex for the postmodern Christian, one that is rooted in the overall story of the Bible, the narrative of God's redeeming love, and humanity's attempt to reflect that love through our institutions and practices. Winner insists that "the only real sex is the sex that happens in a marriage" and to speak about sex or sexual ethics cannot be separated from speaking about marriage. For "the physical coming together that happens between two people who are not married is only a distorted imitation of sex, as Walt Disney's Wilderness Lodge Resort is only a simulation of real wilderness. The danger is that when we spend too much time in the simulations, we lose the capacity to distinguish between the ersatz and the real."[3]

For forty (long) days and nights, our Hollywood hero gives up sexual intercourse outside marriage, or forswears what the Bible calls fornication. As if this, by cultural standards, weren't difficult enough, he adds to the burden a complete abstinence from all sexual activity. His roommate, colleagues, and so-called friends do all they can to hasten Sullivan's breakdown, from setting him up with unwanted dates to leaving porn magazines lying around his apartment to spiking his beverage with Viagra. As the days and weeks progress, the pressure and tensions increase and so do the sexual fantasies and alluring strategies: the one being tempted is haunted by a newly formed vision that enlarges the pleasures that he is missing out on, while the tempters are busying themselves with pointing out and making available what is being missed and could be obtained at a moment's notice.

Underlying this struggle and feeding the hunger for gratification is the concept of ownership and entitlement. In the correspondence of a senior devil in hell named Screwtape to his nephew and spiritual directee, Wormwood, who is an apprentice devil on earth, C. S. Lewis has the senior devil recommend the following practice: "The sense of ownership in general is always to be encouraged. The humans are always putting up claims to ownership which sound equally funny in Heaven and in Hell, and we must keep them doing so." In fact, says Screwtape, "much of the modern resistance to chastity comes from men's belief that they 'own' their bodies—those vast and perilous estates, pulsating with the energy that made the worlds, in which they find themselves without their consent." The point is to produce this sense of ownership not only by pride but also by confusion, and then to teach them not to notice the different senses of the possessive pronoun "mine," which, of course "in its fully possessive sense cannot be uttered by a human being about anything.... They will find out in the end, never fear, to whom their time, their souls, and their bodies really belong—certainly not to *them,* whatever happens."[4]

While temptation and sexual desire is real, the lie is that we own our bodies, hence are entitled to taking matters into our own hands and seeing to it that these desires are being met. C. S. Lewis suggests that even, and especially, the devils know that the only and true owner of our time, soul, and bodies is the One who created them. Meanwhile the Adversary, or Satan, with numerous minions in tow, is using the strategy of suggesting to us that *we* are masters of our souls and bodies, which, by implication, means handing them over to someone other than God, namely, to God's nemesis.

The illusion of being our bodies' owners, along with the suggestive pleasures our bodies might be missing out on, enters our imagination, cushioning our gradual fall like the comfortable loveseat in a dimmed living room or the softness of our mattress.

So what could be the harm in a little flirtatious touch and a kiss? After all, we believe that we can control our bodies, these, as Lewis calls them, "vast and perilous estates, pulsating with the energy that made the worlds." Since kissing and touching isn't sex, we say, and since fantasizing about sex via suggestive gestures or touches or literature isn't either, what's the big deal? The big deal is, to use Winner's words, that such gradual actions of self-gratification and playing with the fire of eros can lead us, step by step, away from relationship and into accepting "the culture's story about sex: that sex is only for fun, that sex has no consequences, that what I do with my body is none of your business, that the goodness of sex is evaluated by the mindblowingness of the orgasm," when the Christian approach to sexual desire is "neither hedonism nor obliteration," but "discipline."[5]

Speaking of discipline, we need to return once more to our protagonist's plight. Having resolved to embark on the spiritual discipline of sexual renunciation, Sullivan is now on his own, while the world composed of his coworkers, friends, and the woman of his dreams, along with his potential but nonfunctional spiritual mentor, are making matters difficult, to say the least. Most disturbing, perhaps, is the failure of a member of the clergy, a church representative, to set the record straight concerning church teachings on sexual activity and the spiritual discipline of sexual abstinence. "Knowing you, you're never gonna make it," the young priest tells Sullivan in parting, like a mocking admonition to get real about the powerful forces of sex — those of his brother as he knows them from long experience and perhaps his own.

My experience with those entrusted with the care of bodies or with the care of souls somewhat mirrors the dismissive posture concerning the celibate life and one's chances of "making it." In the first instance, I had gone to a psychologist at my mother's urging. She was concerned about my psychological health since I had by age twenty-two stopped dating and pursuing a sexual relationship. From my perspective, it was a gradual development. Up until a year earlier, I had been in a relationship, dating one boyfriend for four years and subsequently living with another for three. After the second breakup, it seemed there was little left to be explored and if there was, I was not particularly interested in finding out. Nonetheless, in an effort to please my mother and to perhaps help her (and me) rest assured that there was nothing seriously wrong with my mental condition, I went to see the doctor. During the session, it became clear that the psychologist saw my lacking interest in matters of sex and mating activity as a clear sign of stress, a pathology that needed to be cured and a blemish that, with the right kind of treatment, could be removed in time. I never went back because I did not want to be cured.

That was in Germany. A year later I moved to the United States, and things changed radically. No longer was my lack of interest in dating a liability; it was an asset. Churches were seemingly everywhere, and unlike in my own country, where churches drew only a handful of people (mostly the elderly and those with a predilection for organ and choral concerts), churches in America were filled with people of all age groups who seemed to be listening to what the preacher had to say. I soon started attending church, sometimes two different churches on any given Sunday, and what I heard stunned me. Preachers were telling their flocks, among other things, that sexual immorality, which included living together and having sexual intercourse outside marriage, was wrong in God's sight and would never get you to heaven.

Such a perspective was news to me, but in my present condition, it was good news and a great relief. Not only was I considered "normal" by the church's standards, I thought, but I had become virtuous in one fell swoop. With my newfound certificate of sanity in hand, I felt good about myself, so good in fact that over the next five years the notion grew in me that living the single and celibate life provided immense freedom and was worth keeping. In my ebullience, I shared this intent with a seminary professor, who gave me nothing short of a tongue-lashing. Who did I think I was for attempting to control God or altering God's plan by willful design? To him, people were meant to be married so they could enjoy the God-given gift of sexual fulfillment. Those who refused the gift were in obvious rebellion against God. I had fallen from feeling virtuous to being rebellious by not pursuing marriage so as to be sexually fulfilled.

We have discussed the relatively recent emergence of the theme of romantic love in Western culture; the notion of sexual fulfillment is even more recent, probably beginning with Sigmund Freud's teachings in the early twentieth century. The thesis that all neurosis and psychological disorder is rooted in sexual dissatisfaction and frustration has crept into church teachings and theological discourse on sexual ethics. By buying into the notion of sexual fulfillment as a universal prerequisite for human sanity and wholeness, the church has compromised the doctrine of salvation by grace through faith in Christ, while indirectly saying that those who practice sexual abstinence are "never gonna make it."

A more accurate and theologically sound description of the experience of sexual union would be to call it the "sacrament of sex." The search for one's individual sexual fulfillment is *not* the focus, but instead the mutually redemptive character of sexual activity as a saving action of Christ. In *Against an Infinite Horizon,* Ronald Rolheiser elaborates on the meaning of what he calls sacramental sex: "It has the power to build up the soul in ways that, this side of eternity, few other experiences can. It is Eucharist, incarnation, love-made-flesh ... [where] a soul is joined to another and in that moment experiences the central purpose of God's design for it."[6] With the understanding that sex takes place in the context of marriage, the marriage bed is potentially "a daily eucharist," something "fleshy, tangible, visible, and incarnate" that somehow makes God present. Each time a couple makes love the action is a sacrament that has the potential of expressing "special love, fidelity, reconciliation, and gratitude in an earthy way."[7]

Despite the sacred and sacramental nature of sexual union, there is still that personal space waiting and inviting us to step back into it, to refrain from clinging to any thing or person, and to balance the physical with the spiritual realm. For the physical cannot and never will meet the spiritual need for union. St. Augustine calls our need for union a restlessness of the heart that searches and roams and cannot settle until it finds its ultimate resting place, not in physical union, but in God. Expressing the same principle, Eckhart Tolle sees the root of our physical urge as a spiritual one: the longing for "an end to duality," a return to the state of wholeness. Sexual union, by his definition, "is the closest you can get to this state on the physical level [which is] ... why it is the most deeply satisfying experience the physical realm can offer." But he warns of mistaking this state to be of lasting effect. Sexual union "is no more than a fleeting glimpse of wholeness, an instant of bliss."[8]

As long as we are seeking sexual union as a means of finding wholeness and salvation, we continue to seek an end of duality on the physical level, where it cannot be found. We receive a mesmerizing glimpse of bliss that quickly vanishes, so that we are thrown back on ourselves and the search begins anew. True fulfillment and salvation, or what Jesus calls finding or saving our soul, comes with an awareness that the ultimate union we are made for is union with God. In the solitary encounter of the soul with God, our spirit, contained in the vessel of the human body, meets Spirit. While sexual or bodily union is a foretaste of this divine encounter, it falls short of being its end. Solitude invites us to a principled self-abandon and the "losing of our soul," where we release the imaginary sense of ownership and claim on our bodies and their self-gratification.

Two

Roots of the Spiritual Practice of Solitude

9

The Promise and Price
of Solitude

The biblical narrative of the relationship between God and God's people alternates between promise and price: people pay a price to see the divine promise fulfilled — and not usually with exuberance and a joyous heart. But if they do and after they have "paid up," they find themselves better off — freer than before, unencumbered, made anew. In most instances, the price to be paid is a lesson in sacrifice, a spiritual discipline of letting go. What people think they possess has in actuality usurped God's place in their hearts and possesses them. In the Old Testament, the small and socio-politically insignificant tribe of the Hebrews is singled out and set apart by God to become the living flesh-and-blood witness to surrounding nations and tribes concerning God's presence, God's nature, and God's powers. Not merit on their part, but God's particular ordinance and decree destines the Hebrews, later to be called Israelites, to become both recipient of and witness to God's grace and love.

In a sense, the Israelites are singled out and called on to act as a people singularly different from other nations. They are to act in accordance with what their God asks them to do, not what is the custom of the land. They are to demonstrate their set-apartness by whom they worship and how, as well as by their priorities in marital, commercial, and cultic affairs. They are to marry within the clan, show mercy

to strangers, forgive debtors every seven years, and worship in a place built according to divine specifications. In
short, the Israelites were called out from among the nations
to be separate and distinct so their victories could only be
explained by the God who protected, guided, and strength-
ened them. Much like the Christians later, they were to live
in the world without being of it, rejoicing in their weakness
and dependence upon their God so as to show forth God's
might. They were to welcome strangers and aliens without
being seduced by the lure of their customs and ways.

The earliest biblical account of collective solitude is the
wilderness wandering of the Israelites, recorded in the book
of Exodus. After the Egyptian pharaoh is forced to let the
Hebrews go on account of numerous plagues and Egyptian fatalities, the people are able, by God's miraculous
intervention, to escape across the Red Sea in the direction
of the Promised Land. The promise is both freedom from
bondage under Egyptian rule and their own land that is
flowing "with milk and honey." The price is absolute loyalty
to their God and, by implication, to God's mouthpiece and
appointed leader, Moses, who is charged to lead the expe-
dition. They concur at first, but soon realize how high the
cost is for the promised freedom and land. Not even three
months pass before hunger, thirst, and despair drive them
to voice complaints. "If only we had died by the hand of
the Lord in the land of Egypt, when we sat by the flesh-
pots and ate our fill of bread," they say to Moses, "for you
have brought us out into this wilderness to kill this whole
assembly with hunger" (Exod. 16:3).

On another occasion they experience thirst. Again they
grumble, saying, "Why did you bring us out of Egypt, to kill
us and our children and livestock with thirst?" (Exod. 17:3).
Eventually they grow impatient with their leader and, by
implication, with their God. When Moses was gone for a

long period to commune with God on Mount Sinai, the people gathered around Aaron and said, "Come, make gods for us, who shall go before us; as for this Moses, the man who brought us up out of the land of Egypt, we do not know what has become of him" (Exod. 32:1). After Aaron leads them into constructing a molten calf, the people say about it, "These are your gods, O Israel, who brought you up out of the land of Egypt!" and they worship their new gods and offer up sacrifices (Exod. 32:4–8).

The wilderness experience, the set-apartness and solitude of the Israelites for forty years under prohibitive conditions, brings out the worst in them: they are provoked by thirst and hunger and come close to stoning their leader (Exod. 17:4); they are driven by discontent and look back to their Egyptian captivity as a time of relative ease; and their impatience drives them to shift loyalties from their leader, Moses, and his and their God, who demands a price for protection and deliverance, to a god that comes cheaply, a homemade invention that promises instant gratification and reprieve from the wilderness discomforts.

Being set apart and experiencing solitude comes at a price. The strain is especially apparent at the beginning of the people's journey and at the height of their escape. When the Egyptian armies threaten to overtake the Israelites and their eyes grow wide with fear, they react with cynicism. "Was it because there are no graves in Egypt that you have taken us away to die in the wilderness?" they ask. "For it would have been better for us to serve the Egyptians than to die in the wilderness" (Exod. 14:11, 12b). Moses' reply to the Israelites' despair shortly before the Red Sea crossing is wise counsel in the face of isolation: "Do not be afraid, stand firm, and see the deliverance that the LORD will accomplish for you today" (14:13–14). "The Lord will fight for you, and you have only to keep still" (v. 14b). While thirst

and hunger are real, fear is unwarranted given God's promise to take the people to the Promised Land. Standing firm
means to set or station oneself and accept one's present cir-
cumstances in the wilderness without looking for shortcuts
and escapes; and keeping one's mouth shut or being still
means to pause, to refrain from grumbling and resisting
what cannot be changed at the present. Israel's experience
of collective solitude and set-apartness is a model for our
response to individual solitude and isolation: fear not, embrace the present situation without escape tactics, and be
still—presumably so as to better hear God speak.

The exodus event occupies a central role in biblical
thought as it demonstrates God's action of deliverance.
According to Old Testament scholar Roy Honeycutt, the
prophets made it the basis upon which they appeal to their
generation. The psalmists make reference to it in nearly
twenty psalms as the central motif of Israel's worship. And
the expected endtime reign of the Lord, the coming of the
Messiah, is based on the concept of a new exodus, God's
people once again delivered from bondage to a new type of
freedom. In turn, the New Testament draws heavily on the
theme of exodus, wilderness, and conquest, expressing the
saving work of Christ, or the Messiah, in the vocabulary of
the Israelites' wilderness wanderings. "Redemption," "deliverance," "bondage," and "freedom" are words borrowed
from the Old Testament event. Moreover, the emergence of
Jesus out of Egypt, John the Baptist as "the voice of one crying in the wilderness: Prepare the way of the Lord," the forty
days of temptation in the wilderness, and the similarity between the giving of the Ten Commandments at Sinai and
the Sermon on the Mount all recall the parallels between
the exodus and the life of Jesus.[1] Similarly, the letters of the
Apostle Paul contain about forty references or allusions to
the exodus history.

The place of wilderness solitude is the locus of God's saving action. It is here that the frailty of the faltering human spirit meets the sustaining strength of the divine deliverer. Weakness is pitted against strength, bondage against freedom, and despair against hope. But the human will to fight alone and reject outside intervention and help is not easily subdued. The Israelites cling to what is theirs, most prominently their present emotional upheaval and the memories of the past. In their dilemma of hunger, thirst, and fear of death, they recall with longing an embellished picture of their time in Egypt. They would gladly trade the unknown for the known, the promised freedom they do not understand for the slave labor they do, the future autonomy and independence with God for their past attachments and dependence on surrounding nations. The fact that they are a community, that they have each other for support is more hindrance than help. When one cries out, they all do; when one whimpers, the rest act as choral backup; and when one grumbles, it is magnified into mass dismay. Of course, the Israelites quickly find the visible cause of their discontent. Since they cannot or will not face their own anger and cowardice, they project it onto their leader who, by their account, recklessly abandoned common sense and put them in danger of losing their minds and lives. Meanwhile, they have forgotten God.

Chronologically speaking, solitude precedes salvation. When the exodus narrative is later recounted by the Israelites, it is mostly in the context of worship and the celebration of festivals. But something odd has happened. The distasteful experience of solitude and fear is barely mentioned during the liturgy. The focus is on the salvation event. The Song of Moses in Exodus 15 extols the Lord's strength:

The LORD is a warrior;
the LORD is his name.
Pharaoh's chariots and his army he cast into the sea;
his picked officers were sunk in the Red Sea.
The floods covered them;
they went down into the depths like a stone.
Your right hand, O LORD,
glorious in power—
your right hand, O LORD, shattered the enemy.

(vv. 3–6)

And Psalm 78 retells the exodus event with an emphasis on God's goodness and generosity toward an undeserving, rebellious, and sinful people:

[The Lord] divided the sea and let them pass
    through it,
and made the waters stand like a heap.
In the daytime he led them with a cloud,
and all night long with a fiery light.
He split rocks open in the wilderness,
and gave them drink abundantly as from the deep.
He made streams come out of the rock,
and caused waters to flow down like rivers.
Yet they sinned still more against him,
rebelling against the Most High in the desert.

(vv. 13–17)

The despair and grumbling, the fear and rage, the projecting and the blaming are nearly dropped from memory. People forget the human deprivations and challenges of the wilderness event, along with the attachments and animosities they found deeply lodged within themselves. What they prefer to remember is the experience of divine salvation and deliverance, a God who was in close proximity both night and day and brought those whom God had set apart from bondage into freedom.

The same tendency of omission is at work when I recount my own conversion experience. I notice that I am only too willing to tell of the time, shortly after my coming to the United States from Germany, when I walked into a small Baptist church in rural Georgia, was warmly welcomed and lovingly urged to come back, and heard the preacher speak of God's love for me demonstrated by sending his only son Jesus Christ so I might be saved. Even though I had been raised in church attending weekly Mass, this was the first time I grasped the principal message of the Gospel, the good news about a God who cared by showing supreme love in sacrifice. In my testimony of conversion, I generally concede that I must have been "ripe and ready" to hear and that God had been preparing and softening my heart for some time.

All the while, I am perfectly aware that I am omitting a good portion of what had produced this softening: an intense feeling of loneliness following the breakup of a long-term relationship, a short-changed career in advertising as scruples were mounting about the nature of my work, and a growing sense of alienation and estrangement in Berlin, far away from home, where I had lived for years and where I was constantly surrounded by people—on the subway, in the public parks and museums, along the shopping boulevards — but where I remained an anonymous entity, a stranger in the crowd. To be sure, this extended and discomfiting experience of isolation and solitude, perhaps crisis-like, had preceded my conversion experience and prepared me to be able hear the saving message in Christ.

Likewise, in the exodus narrative, the solitude on Sinai—both the desert and the mountain—creates the context for a heightened awareness of self and God. This is not surprising given the seemingly endless and plain vastness of such a landscape. In his study of desert and mountain spirituality, Belden Lane chronicles his excursions into the deserts and mountain terrains of Australia, New Mexico, and Egypt. He observes the strange effect that these places have on the human spirit. Hostile landscapes of desert and mountain along with thundering clouds, he says, bring us forcibly to the boundaries of what our minds and bodies can endure. They invite "us to the unexplored landscapes of an inner geography where that which is most deeply 'us' is joined to what we experience as radically Other."[2]

Both Sinai desert and mountain are a symbol of "terror and theophany," where Yahweh is encountered in the darkness of unknowing. The spiritual function of such "fierce terrain," says Lane, "is to bring us to the end of ourselves, to the abandonment of language and the relinquishment of ego." And as the vast expanse of jagged stone and sand challenges the intellectual constructs that lend us comfort and pride, we may find that "the things that ignore us save us in the end." As symbols of that great and terrible wilderness, they are a forceful and unrelenting reminder of our "grand inconsequence and the limits of all theological discourse."[3]

In the Hebrew Bible, Yahweh tends to speak to Israel's leaders and prophets mainly when they are alone. Moses is alone when he first receives God's call, and he is alone on Mount Sinai at the time the Ten Commandments and the Torah are given. Amos, like most of the prophets, is a solitary figure, "a herdsman and dresser of sycamore trees," when God reveals the powerful visions that foretell the fate of Israel. And so are many of the other prophets by virtue of their marginal position in Israel, which would sharpen their perception of the injustices suffered by the less fortunate and outsiders. Elijah's call narrative describes how, fleeing Ahab's persecution, this prophet "went a day's journey into the wilderness, and came and sat down under a solitary broom tree" (1 Kings 19:4). The lone tree under which Elijah sits when an angel appears symbolizes his own sense of feeling abandoned and isolated. Later, still alone, Elijah perceives the Lord not in the wind, an earthquake, or fire, but in "a sound of sheer silence" (19:12).

In the New Testament the example of John the Baptist was frequently seen by Christians as a precedent for the ascetic life and withdrawal from society. Jesus led an active social life, but on several occasions the Gospels show him withdrawing from crowds and his disciples in order to rest and pray. He also withdraws to give his disciples special teachings, telling them to "come away to a deserted place all by yourselves and rest a while" (Mark 6:31). Jesus sought seclusion, but "when the crowds found out about it, they followed him; and he welcomed them, and spoke to them about the kingdom of God, and healed those who needed to be cured" (Luke 9:11). Like the prophets, Jesus was aware that the life of faith meant being involved with other people, especially those on the margins of society. He also resembles the prophets in his withdrawal into solitude at crucial moments of his ministry, such as the temptations in the wilderness, the transfiguration scene, and the vigil in the Garden of Gethsemane. In addition, John of Patmos is clearly alone when he receives a series of visions recorded in the book of Revelation, and the Apostle Paul may have spent a number of solitary years between his conversion experience on the Damascus road and the beginning of his preaching ministry (see Gal. 1:17–18).

For us the promise of solitude is a heightened awareness of God's presence, power, and love. The price is the agonizing experience of wilderness terrain, the ominous and unfamiliar surroundings, the uncertainty about the future, the threat to our autonomy and control needs. The promise is hearing the Lord's comforting voice in "a sound of sheer silence" and finding our weakness and fears transformed into strength and hope. The price is confrontation with our cowardice, anger, resentment, and impatience. While the price of solitude is its daunting distress, the promise is a lifegiving transformation so concrete that, in retrospect, we remember and celebrate it as the time when the Lord brought us salvation and deliverance.

10

Solitude as a Christian Lifestyle

Neither the Hebrew Bible nor the New Testament seems to encourage an extended solitary lifestyle. In his overview of the ethics and spirituality of Christian solitude, John D. Barbour points out that the prophets' solitude tended to be temporary. For "the condition of long-term isolation from other people is one viewed with pity or horror in the Hebrew Bible and by most of later Jewish tradition." In order to combat man's isolation, Yahweh makes a woman, for "it is not good that the man should be alone" (Gen. 2:18). Isolation is imposed as a punishment for those who do not observe the Commandments and the Torah. And in many of the Psalms, the speaker laments his loneliness and sense of being an outcast from Israel. Likewise, neither the Gospels nor the Epistles consider solitude as a Christian way of life, except for a specific purpose, such as praying alone to avoid hypocrisy, and for a limited time.[1]

This aversion to solitude changes over the next two hundred years. As an increasing number of men and women committed themselves to the celibate life, their prestige in the Christian body became second only to that of the martyrs. These so-called *continentes,* or celibates, did not at first live in religious communities but in their own homes. They fasted more than other Christians, spent long hours in prayer, lived quietly, dressed modestly, and gave themselves little to commonplace amusements. More and more, the works of charity were entrusted to these celibates. Increasingly they were women, who then as now tended to live longer than men, and who, following their husband's death, found themselves in charge of an estate and holdings. Rather than remarrying someone of lesser fortunes or putting themselves under the auspices of a new husband and "lord," many of these widows (often in their twenties and thirties) dedicated themselves to lifelong celibacy, while setting up house together with other widows and young women of their households, thus marking the beginnings of later convent life. This movement away from conventional family life into small celibate communities was balanced by another movement away from community into solitude.

Christians might have fled from persecution and martyrdom under pagan emperors and sought solitude in hiding. But later, by the end of the third century, in Egypt and Syria a movement of Christians had sprung up for whom solitude became a distinct commitment and spiritual path. The key figure in the desert movement and also in Eastern and Western monasticism was St. Antony. Born in 251 near Memphis in Upper Egypt, he began the solitary life around the year 270 outside his former house, having sold all he possessed and given it to the poor. Fifteen years later, he moved to the tombs outside his village, then to a mountain by the Nile, and later to another mountain by the Red Sea. All in all, St. Antony is said to have lived in solitude for nearly eighty years, dying in 356.

A shift in attitude occurred soon after Christianity was recognized as the official religion of the Roman Empire following the conversion of Constantine in 312. One of the primary impulses behind the growing desire for solitude was the wish to disconnect from the temptations in the increasingly worldly success of the church. According to Laura Swan, O.S.B., many Christians "experienced a conflict between the growing power associated with the institutionalization of the church and the pursuit of holiness. Christianity's move from the margins of society and from the home to the dominant strata of society and the public basilica left some believers feeling that Christianity was compromised," losing its prophetic character for the sake of "convenience and political expedience."[2] In addition, theological disputes ravaged the church and unsettled the life of believers.

Meanwhile, the early desert Christians, following in the footsteps of St. Antony, believed that it was not possible to lead a fully Christian life in the social, economic, and theological upheaval of the late Roman Empire. By 325, the time of the Council of Nicea, there were over five thousand solitaries, women as well as men, in the desert of Nitria, Egypt. First they were simply hermits living alone but meeting on Saturday and Sunday in some central place for the Eucharist. Shortly before Nicea, Pachomius (b. 292) had devised something approaching a monastery rule. By the time he died in 348, there were eight or nine such groups subject to him totaling in the thousands, and fifty years later, there were fifty thousand living in this kind of organization.[3] These solitaries were called hermits, from the Greek word *eremos,* desert.

Serving as inspiration for the desert fathers and mothers were the Israelites' wilderness wanderings of the exodus, the call episodes of the prophets, and the accounts of John the Baptist and Jesus in the wilderness. A lifestyle of silence, simplicity, and solitude directed their work, study, and prayer. Speech was sparse so as to redirect every aspect of body, mind, and inner world toward God. Cultivating simplicity involved not only modesty in speech, meals, and dress, but also simplicity and balance of emotion, a detachment from people and things, and intentionality about one's activities. According to Henri Nouwen, the hermits sought to free themselves from the "compulsive self, to shake off the many layers of self-deception and reclaim their true self. In the desert, away from human praise and criticism, they could slowly grow into the knowledge that they are not who people say they are...; that as long as they kept trying to find their identity outside of God, they ended up in that vicious spiral of wanting more and more."[4] Solitude, especially in one's cell, was considered the place for spiritual combat in which one examined one's true self, thus gaining a deepened awareness of personal sin. According to Swan, if "the ascetic could not find God in the cell, then she would not find God elsewhere."[5] Such solitude could be practiced by cultivating a sense of detachment and self-awareness even when moving back and forth between the monastic community and the desert, between contact with others and the cell's isolation. One of the contemporary scholars on desert spirituality and history, Benedicta Ward, S.L.G., says that "the inner world of detachment from self and freedom of heart towards God" was central. An elder would advise the novice, "Let this be a sign to you of progress in the virtues when you have acquired mastery of the passions and the appetites." Another would say, "We often see laypeople abstaining from pleasures for the sake of their health or for some other rational motive. How much more should the monk take care of the health of his soul and his mind and his spirit."[6]

The desert was not a pastoral retreat, but a place of harsh conditions where survival was difficult. Often the chosen location was characterized by strong winds, wild animals, and minimal necessities, so that the dwellers were in close proximity with the forces of nature. The desert came to be understood as a place of death — the place where one died to the false self, and where one encountered the realm of the spiritual and the demonic. Demons figured prominently in all desert literature. One of the desert elders, Evagrius Ponticus (345–99), a prolific writer and theologian, suggests that demons attack different people in different ways. They attack people of the world "chiefly through their deeds"; they attack monks living in community chiefly through the irritating habits of their brothers; and they attack the desert solitaries "by means of thoughts." "Just as it is easier to sin by thought than by deed," says Evagrius, "so also is the war fought on the field of thought more severe than that which is conducted in the area of things and events."[7] According to Evagrius, one of the fiercest demons is *acedia*, translated as listlessness, boredom, or gloom. The only solution to its cure is to stay put in one's cell, to "stay seated inside and be patient and receive nobly the attackers." To leave one's cell is to climb out of the "boxing ring" or desert "the wrestling match" in the middle of the fight; and "to flee such struggles and to avoid them teaches the mind to be unskilled and lazy and fugitive."[8]

The desert fathers and mothers were the inspiration for the church's season of Lent. In the fourth century, bishops visited these solitaries living in caves in the wilderness of Egypt and were inspired by the visible, joyous witness of Christian discipleship. They wanted members of their parishes to catch a glimpse of the healing power of the solitary life. And since they could not arrange for caravans to bring all the people out into the wilderness, they resolved to bring the wilderness to them: For forty days prior to Easter, parishioners would enter wilderness territory, not out in the desert of Egypt but in their own familiar surroundings through a Lenten discipline, marked by abstinence. Fasting, simplicity, and silence were to reconstruct the austere and fierce conditions of wilderness living. And instead of wrestling the demons in caves and monastic cells, believers would be setting foot in the cave of their soul. By eating less, doing less, and doing with less, they were brought face-to-face with the powers and demons that owned them, the habits that controlled them, and the possessions and attachments that had taken precedence over the place of God in Christ.

II

The Cost of Discipleship

Central to the desert ascetics' practice and the vows of commitment of later monastics in the West is a passage on the nature of discipleship in the Gospel of Luke. Near the end of

Jesus' earthly ministry, the Gospel writer tells us that "large crowds were traveling with him." These crowds apparently had joined the movement without being aware of the cost. Abruptly Jesus turns to them and says, "Whoever comes to me and does not hate father and mother, wife and children, brothers and sisters, yes, and even life itself, cannot be my disciple. Whoever does not carry the cross and follow me cannot be my disciple" (Luke 14:26–27; cf. Matt. 10:34–39). The passage is a reminder that we are on our own when it comes to making a decision to follow Christ. We cannot ride into Christian discipleship on the coattails of our parents, our spouse, our children, our siblings. As evangelist Benny Hinn tells audiences, "God has no grandchildren," only children — sons and daughters, birthed by the Spirit in a solitary one-on-one encounter with Christ. Or as the Gospel of John says concerning Jesus, "to all who received him, who believed in his name, he gave power to become children of God" (John 1:12).

In the Christian classic *The Cost of Discipleship*, Dietrich Bonhoeffer comments on the Luke passage and highlights the solitary nature of discipleship. People "are frightened of solitude, and they try to protect themselves from it by merging themselves in the society of their fellow-men and in their material environment." In short, "they are unwilling to stand alone before Jesus and to be compelled to decide with their eyes fixed on him alone."[1] This call of Jesus, says Bonhoeffer, teaches us "that our relation to the world has been built on an illusion." All this time we may have been thinking we had a direct relationship with other people, especially members of our own family or our spouse. Now we find out that these relationships are in fact what hinder us from faith and obedience. Even "in the most intimate relationships of life, in our kinship with father and mother, brothers and sisters, in married love, and in our duty to the community, direct relationships are impossible." By the coming of Christ and his call and claim, "his followers have no more immediate realities of their own," regardless of whether they realize it or not. Between others and ourselves "stands Christ the Mediator." This means in effect that we "are separated from one another by an unbridgeable gulf of otherness and strangeness which resists all our attempts to overcome it by means of natural association or emotional or spiritual union." And wherever a group, "be it large or small, prevents us from standing alone before Christ, wherever such a group raises a claim of immediacy [on us] it must be hated for the sake of Christ."[2]

According to Bonhoeffer, the breach with all our immediate relationships on account of Christian discipleship is "inescapable." It may take the form of an external and open breach, with family or nation, for example; or it may take the form of an initially "hidden and a secret breach" that will become visible and plain in time. Abraham, says Bonhoeffer, is an example of both. He first had to leave his friends and his father's house and become a stranger and sojourner in order to gain the Promised Land. Later on, he was called by God to offer his own son Isaac as a sacrifice when "Christ had come between the father of faith and the child of promise," so Abraham could "learn that the promise did not depend on Isaac, but on God alone."[3]

To understand God's call to Abraham to "hate" and sacrifice his only son, we have to backtrack a little. "Do not be afraid, Abram," the Lord had said at least fifteen years earlier. "I am your shield; your reward shall be very great. . . . Look toward heaven and count the stars, if you are able to count them. . . . So shall your descendants be" (Gen. 15:1, 5). But since descendents required children, and since there wasn't a single child, and Abraham and Sarah were nearly eighty and ninety, respectively, the promise seemed odd.

Still each month they hoped and they prayed, each year they did, until it was a full ten years later. Impatient (an understatement!) with seeing the divine vision come to pass, Abraham was more than willing to follow his wife's suggestion: Go ahead and sleep with my housekeeper, she says to him, perhaps this will get us the promised children (Gen. 16:2).

From a legal perspective, there was no problem with that in ancient Israel, since children born of slaves and fathered by their masters were considered the master's legal offspring. But from a moral perspective there was. Despite the practice of polygamy in Canaan, the Mosaic teachings did not endorse polygamy for Hebrews, and the sacred covenant between man and woman mentioned in Genesis 2 remained fully in effect in Genesis 22. What was legally valid was still morally wrong. The narrator of the story is quite aware of this, since he tries to keep Abraham's nose clean. It is predictable who gets pinned with the immoral act: the woman. Much like the story of the Fall where Eve induces Adam to eat of the forbidden fruit and Adam "innocently" succumbs, Sarah suggests the ill-advised deed to Abraham who merely "does what he is told." Nevertheless, it soon becomes clear in each case that both parties, man and woman, bear equal responsibility for the misdeed, and both end up paying the price.

The ramifications of the latter couple's disobedience to God are numerous. Sarah is jealous of her servant girl, Abraham is paralyzed by the hatred between the two women, and Abraham and Sarah are at marital odds. The irony is that in the midst of all this chaos, God makes good on a promise made ten years before. Sarah is ninety when she gives birth to Isaac. And with the arrival of the real heir, the proxy child, Ishmael—prematurely conceived and born to Hagar the servant — is no longer needed. It is only a matter of time before Hagar falls into disgrace, loses her livelihood, and is driven off by Abraham into the wilderness of Beersheba, where her son, due to lack of water, nearly dies. These are the ramifications of sin. Abraham, along with Sarah, had been unwilling to wait for God. They had forced the hand of providence, greedily reaching for the next-best thing, while harming human dignity and putting lives at risk.

We can only imagine Abraham's emotional attachment to his son Isaac. And we don't need to question Abraham's qualities as a father or faithful provider. What we need to question is this: To what degree did Abraham see his son as the extension of his own unfulfilled dreams? Would he continue to use him, as he did Hagar, as a means to an end? Or would he do better next time around? Apparently, these are the questions that God has, too, and maybe even Abraham himself. And so to test the purity of Abraham's motives, God demands the ultimate sacrifice. "Take your son, your only son Isaac, whom you love, and go to the land of Moriah, and offer him there as a burnt offering on one of the mountains that I shall show you" (Gen. 22:2). And without the slightest hint of hesitation — almost as if he knew this challenge to be a second chance with God, Abraham obeys. He rose early, saddled his donkey, and took along two of his servants, with Isaac in tow. After a three-day journey, he told his servants to stay back and took his son with him. There, alone and secluded, Abraham built an altar, arranging the wood, binding his son like a burnt offering, and placing him on the woodpile. And when the knife is poised, Abraham demonstrates that this time he is heeding God's plan. No more manipulating and maneuvering. He is willing to part with the one earthly possession that could take him to his place of desire. And because he is willing,

God stays the hand, providing a ram in Isaac's stead, and renewing the promise from long ago.

Like Abraham, we too are held captive by our desires and dreams. They become an obstacle between us and God, between the illusionary image we cherish of ourselves and the one God made of us in Christ. In the hymn "A Mighty Fortress Is Our God," Martin Luther speaks to his contemporaries of the sixteenth century, as well as to us: "Let goods and kindred go, this mortal life also; the body they may kill, God's truth abideth still, His kingdom is forever." Letting go of kindred and goods, even our mortal body and our concern for it, relinquishing their claims on us as a means to an end, implies that we are placing ourselves before God naked and utterly alone with nothing in between.

In his earthly ministry, Jesus rejects the claims of family on himself, while preaching about a new family, one not based on flesh and blood. "Whoever does the will of God is my brother and sister and mother" (Mark 3:35), he tells those who had come reporting that his mother and brothers were standing outside and expecting to see him. But this is not said in an effort to enlarge upon his newly forming circle of followers. According to Sandra M. Schneiders, I.H.M., "Jesus does not establish a 'spiritual family' of which he is head, but includes himself in a transcendent family of which God alone is the head."[4] To underscore this new reality, Jesus draws to himself a group of people — those he calls and those who call on him and whom he allows to come along. Not "blood or obligation," not "ancestry or biology," but "a free personal autonomy" in choosing to make a commitment to God in Christ are the unifying factor. "This community," says Schneiders, "which later called itself 'Church,' was to be the seed, the realization in this world, of a whole new order that Jesus called the Reign of God."[5]

So what does Jesus mean when he says that "whoever does not carry the cross and follow me cannot be my disciple"? Is the cross the letting go of our attachments to goods and kindred? Is it the little small deaths we die with each illusion crushed, with each stark nothingness endured, with each disturbing silence met? In a sermon on the Luke passage, Barbara Brown Taylor says that the cross is the saving tool of Christ. Jesus "is always offering to share it with us, to let us get underneath it with him. Not, I think, because he wants us to suffer but because he wants us to know how alive you can feel even underneath something that heavy and how it can take your breath away to get hold of your one true necessity."[6]

The cross on which Jesus was crucified is both a historical reality and a metaphor of his death — and yours and mine. As a metaphor, it paints a picture of pain, abandonment, and death in utter isolation. It invites us to linger there long enough to acknowledge what is false and untrue in our motives and ambitions — and what needs to die. It is also a reality, for as we first embark upon discipleship we surrender ourselves to Christ in union with his death. In Bonhoeffer's words, "It may be a death like that of the first disciples who had to leave home and work to follow him, or it may be a death like Luther's, who had to leave the monastery and go out into the world." Ultimately "every command of Jesus is a call to die, with all our affections and lusts."[7] With its force of cruel reality, the cross compels us to scrutinize our affections, attachments, and passions; the strength and power we derive from our relations and connections; and the priorities we give to what lies outside us. Thus, daily it beckons us to let go and join Christ in death anew. What the cross does not spell out is the other side of death — the new and liberating life that springs from it after it has forced us, when everything else is seemingly gone, "to get hold of our one true necessity." This is the cost, and the reward, of discipleship.

12

One True Necessity

The early Christians experimented with finding ways of detachment and solitude — toward standing before God unencumbered and naked, as it were. They knew that solitude preceded salvation, that weakness preceded strength, that the experience of aloneness preceded finding communion in the transcendental family of faith in Christ. Among the ways of detachment were a deliberate commitment to poverty and simplicity of lifestyle, a guarded celibacy for the unmarried — and even the married — and obedience to the elders of their faith community and the rule of Christ. The ultimate solitary encounter with God in Christ was martyrdom, surrendering to death, rather than compromising on one's faith when pressured by civic and magisterial authorities. Christians died for their convictions, not always because they could not escape the authorities, but because they saw their resolve to fully detach from this earthly life and to cling to their "one true necessity" — Christ—as the ultimate test of discipleship.

The earliest accounts of Christian martyrdom come from the mid-second century, describing the trials and deaths of Ignatius (35–107), Polycarp (69–155), and Justin Martyr

(100–165). In his introduction to the epistle of the martyrdom of Polycarp, bishop of Smyrna, A. Cleveland Coxe
characterizes the account as "evidence of the strength of
Christ perfected in human weakness, thus giving us assurance of grace for our days in every time of need." To be sure,
the details of martyrdom stories, including this one, are re-
pulsive because of their bloodshed and violence. "When I
see in it, however," says Coxe, "an example of what a noble
army of martyrs, women and children included, suffered in
those days 'for the testimony of Jesus,' and in order to hand
down the knowledge of the Gospel to these boastful ages of
our own, I confess myself edified by what I read." In short,
"I am humbled and abashed in comparing what a Christian used to be, with what a Christian is, in our times, even
at his best estate."[1]

The account of Polycarp's martyrdom is possibly the earliest of Christian martyr stories. It is reported to have been
based on a copy handed down by Irenaeus (130–200),
bishop of Lyons and a disciple of Polycarp's, and it pon-
ders preceding martyrdoms of Christians: "Who can fail to
admire their nobleness of mind, and their patience, with
that love towards their Lord which they displayed? — who,
when they were so torn with scourges, that the frame of
their bodies, even to the very inward veins and arteries,
was laid open, still patiently endured, while even those that
stood by pitied and bewailed them."[2] They were so self-
contained, the letter writer reports, "that not one of them
let a sigh or a groan escape them; thus proving to us all
that those holy martyrs of Christ, at the very time when
they suffered such torments, were absent from the body, or
rather, that the Lord then stood by them, and communed
with them." Consequently "they despised all the torments
of this world" by keeping before their eye the fire of eternal
judgment from which they redeemed themselves "by [the

suffering of] a single hour" and "looked forward with the eyes of their heart to those good things which are laid up for such as endure."[3]

Here is an excerpt of the exchanges between the civic authorities at Smyrna and the bishop of Smyrna, most of it taking place in a large stadium filled with people clamoring to see the bloodshed.

> AUTHORITIES: "What harm is there in saying, Lord Caesar, and in sacrificing, with the other ceremonies observed on such occasions, and so make sure of safety?"

> POLYCARP: "I shall not do as you advise me."

Due to Polycarp's refusal, the officials throw him off the carriage that was taking him to the stadium and he dislocates his leg by the fall. Without "being disturbed and as if suffering nothing, he walks speedily" and is escorted into the crowded stadium.

> AUTHORITIES: "Swear by the fortune of Caesar, and I shall set you free; reproach Christ."

> POLYCARP: "Eighty and six years have I served him, and he never did me any injury: how then can I blaspheme my King and Savior?"

> AUTHORITIES: "I have wild beasts at hand: to these I will throw you, unless you repent."

> POLYCARP: "Call them then, for we are not accustomed to repent of what is good in order to adopt that which is evil."

> AUTHORITIES: "I will set you on fire, unless you repent."

> POLYCARP: "You threaten me with fire that burns for an hour and then is extinguished, but you are ignorant of

the fire of the coming judgment and of eternal punishment reserved for the ungodly. What are you waiting for? Do as you intend."[4]

Thereupon Polycarp is roped and placed on the woodpile to be burned. His eyes are turned to heaven and he prays to the Lord in gratitude: "I give you thanks that you have counted me worthy of this day and this hour, that I should have a part of your martyrs, of the cup of your Christ, to the resurrection of eternal life, both of soul and body, through the incorruption imparted by the Holy Spirit."[5]

Around 200 C.E., Clement, a Greek theologian and head of the Christian school in Alexandria, comments on martyrdom in his *Stromateis* ("The Miscellanies"). According to Clement, there are three audiences the martyr addresses. "The martyr bears witness" of being faithful and loyal toward God before others; to the tempter of having in vain shown envy toward the one who is faithful in love; and to the Lord of the persuasion of the truth of His doctrines from which the martyr will not depart through fear of death. For Clement, martyrdom is the supreme act of perfection for it constitutes the "perfect work of love."[6] But there is another type of martyrdom as well — the spiritual one. Each soul that lived purely in the knowledge of God and obeyed the commandments is a witness both by life and word, regardless of the way in which a person dies or the soul "may be released from the body." This person, says Clement, sheds "faith as blood." For "whoever shall leave father, or mother, or brethren" for the sake of the gospel and Jesus' name is blessed, not by an actual martyrdom but by a spiritual one, and by the leaving of "worldly kindred, and wealth, and every possession, in order to lead a life free from passion."[7]

By the third and early fourth centuries, martyrdom is closely linked with another solitary practice, virginity or celibacy. The earliest teachers of the church, the church fathers, argue that celibacy will empower Christians to die fearlessly for their faith and convictions—as indeed many did following the persecutions of 248 under Emperor Decian and of 303 under Emperor Diocletian. As examples of such fearless resolve in the face of death, they identify men and women who fit two criteria: they never married, and they were killed. The Fathers' inspiration may have come in part from a poetic dialogue written around 300 C.E. by Methodius of Olympus (260–312). The dialogue is called "The Banquet of the Ten Virgins" or "Concerning Chastity," but due to the work's similarity to Plato's, it became known as "The Symposium."[8] This Symposium, instead of portraying a gathering of sexually active men, features a study circle of ten women gathered at a banquet, celebrating their sexual abstinence and arguing the reasons for their resolve. The role of Socrates as teacher of philosophy falls to Thecla, the heroine of the second-century *Apocryphal Acts of Paul and Thecla*—a coworker with the apostle Paul, a prophetess and evangelist, and a lifelong celibate.

Toward the end of the banquet, Thecla leads the choir of virgins in a responsorial hymn of thanksgiving. The hymn is set to the parable of the ten virgins and praises certain biblical characters for their virtues of bodily or spiritual martyrdom and sexual renunciation. These characters are Abel, who prefigures Jesus' martyrdom; Joseph, who repels the sexual advances of Potiphar's wife; Jephthah's daughter, who as a virgin is "slaughtered" and offered up like a lamb; Judith, a widow, who cunningly employs the sexual interest of Holofernes, commander of the Assyrian army, to cut off his head and thus deliver her people; Susanna, a married woman, who would rather die than have sexual intercourse with the two judges who pressure her to do so; John the Baptist, who was "led to slaughter" because of his indictment of Herod, who had broken up his brother's marriage; and the Virgin Mary, who was suspected of premarital intercourse on account of Jesus' birth. While Thecla cantors the twenty-four-verse hymn, the choir responds with, "I keep myself pure for Thee, O Bridegroom, and holding a lighted torch I go to meet Thee." Two themes stand out in the hymn. First, the virgins have left family and home for the sake of Christ. Second, the hymn praises martyrdom as a means of preserving one's virginity from violent male aggressors.

Celibacy as a practice of solitude and the context for a heightened reliance on God in Christ was an early development among Christians.[9] By 200 C.E., the church had begun to actively encourage both women and men to practice sexual abstinence both within and apart from marriage and had begun attaching less merit to motherhood. Along with increasing numbers of men and women remaining single and celibate by taking vows, the order of widows had sprung up in various Christian communities. These widows, along with some widowers, included not only the old, poor, and needy who were left without family ties or a source of income following the death of their spouse, but many younger, educated, and wealthy members, who may have joined the order with the prospect of spending the rest of their lives in the service of the church.

According to historian Peter Brown, prominent Christian men and women began using "their bodies to mock continuity through the drastic gesture of perpetual chastity," thereby announcing the imminent approach of a "new creation."[10] Such a practice contrasted with the policies of the

Roman government, for example, which penalized the un-married and childless for the first three centuries of the Christian era, as well as widows and divorced women who failed to remarry within two years. But it also conflicted with Judaism and its high praise of marriage upon which rested the continuity and survival of Israel. While the rabbis were aware of and tolerated some ascetic practices of more recent Judaic origins, they felt it was better that all people abstained from sexual intercourse for some time than for some people to abstain from it all the time.

Celibacy among the early Christians is a distinct expres-sion of a general attitude that detaches from and rejects the world. This general attitude is encapsulated in the sayings of Jesus in the Gospels regarding the disciple's relationship with father and mother, brother and sister, children and spouse. It also emerges in the sayings concerning home, possessions, and wealth both in the Sermon on the Mount and in Jesus' encounters with people unable to part with what they own or with what owns them in order to fol-low him.

Thus, celibacy opens up an alternative to married life and, as all alternatives do, creates a freedom of choice and a vacuum. Physical attachment and bodily union is suspended and God is invited to step into their place. In ad-dition, celibacy implies a detachment from physical ties to family, possessions, and social obligations. By renouncing the quest for physical union and a family of one's own, one relinquishes the ties of family responsibility and ownership. By breaking with the world of matter and the flesh, the be-liever becomes a solitary, one who is free to pursue a new kingdom reality and the "one necessity" in Christ.

13

Living by the Rule

Tentative ways of preparing the context and the vacuum for God to enter into one's solitude soon became regulative vows. By 200 C.E., celibacy was established among Christians as the ideal preferred over marriage. Many, though still a minority, renounced not only marriage but possessions and lived a life devoted to prayer and works of mercy. The practice of celibate living for both men and women had gained acclaim especially among the more affluent members of the Christian faith. The order of widows had been well established and virgins consecrated themselves to perpetual virginity, while mostly living at home. In Spain, for example, the Council of Elvira (c. 306) drew up regulations concerning virgins living at home, which indicates how widespread the practice had become. By the third century, various communities of celibate men and women, usually living in separate quarters, had sprung up in both East and West, largely owing to the difficulties of living a celibate life in the context of home and family.

At the same time, the practice of men and women who were not related and living together under the same roof was viewed with suspicion. Responding to the question of cohabitation among celibates — in this case virgins living in the same house as their deacon or presbyter — Cyprian (200–258), bishop of Carthage, writes in a letter dating from about 250 (Epistle 61): "No one who is near to danger is long safe, nor will the servant of God be able to escape the devil if he has entangled himself in the devil's nets. We must interfere at once with such as these, that they may be separated while yet they can be separated in innocence; because by and by they will not be able to be separated by our interference, after they have become joined together by a very guilty conscience."[1] Apparently the practice of celibate cohabitation had become fairly popular.

By the beginning of the fourth century, some of the celibate communities — starting with those in the East under Pachomius and then spreading to the West—had organized themselves under a communal rule and ordering principles that involved special clothing and a common purse. Among the most widely enduring monastic rules in the West is the one written by Benedict of Nursia (480–543). Benedict, often called the father of Western monasticism, took his inspiration from several existing rules of East and West. In addition, Benedict was familiar with *The Life of Antony* and the collected sayings of the desert fathers and mothers. Following studies in Rome and repelled by the immorality he saw, Benedict renounced the world to become a hermit living in solitude in a cave near the city. After years of ascetic life, Benedict was asked by nearby monks to become their abbot, but when they found his attempts to reform them too rigorous, they tried to poison him. Once again he returned to life as a hermit, and his fame as an ascetic began to attract numerous other disciples, who formed twelve monasteries. Due to conflict with local clergy, Benedict moved to Monte Cassino, where he founded a monastery and wrote his famous rule between 530 and 540.[2]

The life conceived by Benedict is that of a community of people who live together in one place under the direction of their abbot and are relatively free from outside interference. The rule, consisting of a prologue and seventy-three chapters, regulates community life in the spirit of moderation and cooperation. In the prologue Benedict says, "We hope to ordain nothing harsh, nothing burdensome," so that excessive austerities, such as penances or extended fasts, were not permitted. The rule was written, in Benedict's words, "for beginners" and ordinary people, not for extraordinary spiritual athletes. Its purpose was to establish "a school for the Lord's service," a place where monks could learn to serve the Lord in obedience to their abbot, Christ's representative, and "run on the path of God's commandments" with "hearts overflowing with...love."[3]

I saw what such a life entails when, during my seminary education, I took a course at a Benedictine monastery and seminary, St. Meinrad in Indiana. Most of my classmates were studying for the priesthood and served as a guide to this bewildered outsider, who was a Southern Baptist seminarian from Germany studying to become a pastor. Together we went to morning and evening prayers, ate supper with the monks, and shared a table in the library. On my last day, the abbot gave me a gift: the Rule of St. Benedict. I should study it, he said, as it was a guide to living, not just for monks but for everyone wanting to live life for God, longing to be God's servant and finding the joy that is in Christ. Back home in my dorm room, I would open the Rule, underlining passages that stood out, and consulting my English-German dictionary for words whose meaning escaped me. It soon became clear that there was a lot more than just words I didn't understand. The entire concept of living in community under the abbot's authority, praying and singing at all hours of the day, working at no pay, and being kind and cheerful—which they all certainly had been — seemed otherworldly. It troubled me, it fascinated me, and it frightened me. What if I, too, should hear the call from God to a life of poverty, celibacy, and obedience?

And if this call came, what exactly would be the stumbling blocks and the hardest things to let go of?

A few years earlier I had come to this country to do graduate work. All my earthly necessities had been crammed into three suitcases, and not much had been added since. My dorm room at the seminary held books borrowed from the library, spiral notebooks, a typewriter, and an assortment of clothes that were mostly secondhand. The Rule said that "no one may presume to give, receive or retain anything as his own, nothing at all — not a book, writing tablets or stylus — in short, not a single item, especially since monks may not have the free disposal even of their own bodies and wills" (C 33). The year after I had read the Rule I went back to Germany to sell at a flea market what I had been storing in the attic of my parents' home — books mostly, and an array of artwork and antique toys acquired during my college years of collector's craze. "How could you part with these gorgeous things?" the eager buyers would ask as soon as the deals were completed. And to my surprise I heard myself saying that these things were weighing me down in living a life for God.

My little booklet of St. Benedict's Rule bears a few margin notes and underlined phrases. There is also an exclamation point next to the chapter heading titled "obedience." It must have caught my eye back then because it seemed a hard thing at the time, and still is: submitting to someone whose authority rested with a title and position, the abbot. Benedict had taken great care in outlining the numerous qualifications for the candidate of abbot: The abbot is believed to hold the place of Christ in the monastery, he wrote. Therefore, he "will bear the blame wherever the father of the household finds that the sheep have yielded no profit." He must point out to the disciples all that is good and holy more by example than by words, proposing the commandments

of the Lord to receptive disciples with words, but demon-
strating God's instructions to the stubborn and the dull by
a living example. The abbot must know what a difficult
and demanding burden he has undertaken: directing souls
and serving a variety of temperaments, coaxing, reproving, and encouraging them as appropriate. Above all, he
must not show too great concern for the fleeting and temporal things of this world, neglecting or treating lightly the
welfare of those entrusted to him (C 2).

All this would be well and good if indeed the one in authority held these qualifications. But what if intelligence,
competence, and wisdom were lacking? What if one should
disagree with the decisions the abbot had reached? Obedience, says Benedict, is not to be dependent upon a constant
evaluation of the qualifications displayed by the one in
authority, but is a result of one's own humility. Disciples
practicing humility no longer live by their own judgment,
giving in to their whims and appetites; rather they walk according to another's decisions and directions, choosing to
live in monasteries and to have an abbot over them (C 5).

As in modern twelve-step programs, Benedict outlines
twelve steps toward humility, leading to perfect obedience—and to perfect love. Through this love, says Benedict,
all that the disciple "once performed with dread, he will
now begin to observe without effort, as though naturally,
from habit, no longer out of fear of hell, but out of love for
Christ, good habit and delight in virtue" (C 7). And since
Benedict apparently knew both himself and the human
condition well, he repeatedly focuses on the one stumbling
block to obedience: grumbling. For obedience "will be ac-
ceptable to God and agreeable to men only if compliance
with what is commanded is not cringing or sluggish or
half-hearted, but free from any grumbling or any reaction

of unwillingness." After all, the obedience shown to superiors is as if it were given to God. And if "a disciple obeys grudgingly and grumbles, not only aloud but also in his heart, then, even though he carries out the order, his action will not be accepted with favor with God, who sees that he is grumbling in his heart" and will offer no reward for service of this kind, but "punishment for grumbling" (C 5). So then, says Benedict, "Obey the orders of the abbot unreservedly, even if his own conduct—which God forbid—be at odds with what he says. [And] do not grumble or speak ill of others" (C 4). In this way, the recognition of an authority outside myself puts in chains the raging drive to control my life and to assume power over it.

Poverty is the letting go of goods seemingly placed in our care. Obedience is a conscious resolve of placing oneself, without grumbling, into the hands of God. Both acts are thoroughly countercultural, paying virtually no heed to what we have learned in growing up: you are what you have and appear to possess, and you are entitled to celebrating and exhibiting your independence, your critical thinking, and your freedom of choice. Despite the communal practice of poverty and obedience, both acts are solitary endeavors: both continually invite the conscience to strip naked of outer adornments and to displace one's self-will; both invite the disciple to continually pause and inspect the subtle ties of passion, preference, and judgment that might be forming and to cut them so as to create a vacuum for God.

Today most of the monastic communities in the West are marked by three vows that members profess during the ceremony of consecration: the vows of poverty, celibacy (or chastity), and obedience. The *Catechism of the Catholic Church* calls these vows the "evangelical counsels." Christ, the catechism says, "proposes the evangelical counsels, in their great variety, to every disciple." But those who have freely responded to the calling to the consecrated life in religious community are under "obligation of practicing chastity in celibacy for the sake of the Kingdom, [along with] poverty and obedience." This practice, says the catechism, goes back to the very beginning of the church, where "there were men and women who set out to follow Christ with greater liberty, and to imitate him more closely, by practicing the evangelical counsels. They led lives dedicated to God, each in his own way. [And] many of them, under the inspiration of the Holy Spirit, became hermits or founded religious families."[4]

Benedict's rule does not spell out celibacy as a separate vow. It is implied in one's lifestyle and overall commitment to Christ. "Live by God's commandments every day; treasure chastity, harbor neither hatred nor jealousy of anyone, and do nothing out of envy" (C 4:63–67). According to Benedictine scholar and monastic Joan Chittister, O.S.B., celibacy is "the public declaration that the monastic will belong to everyone and to no one at the same time. Celibacy says that human community is built on a great deal more than the sexual, that it transcends sexual love, and pours itself out with no expectation of outpouring in return." In that sense, "Benedictine spirituality calls for love in breadth and love in depth and love in human, rather than simply sexual, terms." It says that "each of us is whole before God, that God has absolute priority for us, that God is sufficient for us, and that God's demands over our lives are total." All people, whether single, married, or monastic, "have this same call to ultimate aloneness and ultimate union with God."[5] For those of us outside the monastery, the call to such aloneness and union with God may be less pronounced. We may even be frightened when confronted by it through the example of monastic discipline and life. However, the call to solitude and separation and celibate self-abandon can come to anyone, and does in time, and with it the invitation of finding one's wholeness in God alone.

Benedictines are fond of saying that they, unlike other religious orders, have a fourth vow. It is the vow of stability, the promise to remain for life with the same community in time and place. Benedict wanted to counter a common practice among some monks, whom he calls *gyrovagues,* who were swapping one community for another, ever looking for a better fit. They "spend their entire lives drifting from region to region, staying as guests for three or four days in different monasteries. Always on the move, they never settle down, and are slaves to their own wills and gross appetites." To Benedict, they "are worse than *sarabaites,*" those who with no experience and rule to guide them, "have a character as soft as lead" and "are the most despicable kind of monks" (C 1).

Stability, says Chittister, is "the willingness to continue to grow where I am." For "someday, somehow I have to see a thing through to the end or I will never come to know what I was meant to find there and I will never come to recognize the face of God that is hidden there and I will never come to be all that I could be there." The commitment to stability means that leaving a place at the drop of a hat when things are not going my way is not an option. It thereby produces a "grace that comes from anger suffered but not spat out, or pain borne but not denied."[6] According to Esther de Waal, scholar of Benedictine spirituality, stability puts an end to "the bewildering and exhausting rushing from one thing" and one place to another. "The man or woman who voluntarily limits herself or himself to one building and a few acres of ground for the rest of life," she says, "is saying that contentment and fulfillment do not consist in constant change, that true happiness cannot necessarily be found anywhere other than in this place and this time."[7]

Stability is more concerned with people than place. It means accepting God's plan that participating in the mystery of Christ happens through *this* particular family and no other. Having to see the same people, day in and day out, coping with their foibles and idiosyncrasies without the easy option of leaving them behind, requires a certain caution in how we treat them. Our discontent and displeasure will bear fruit that we end up reaping. We cannot escape the consequences of our actions. The mirror stays ever before us of what we have said to others, how we have treated them, and how they will respond.

Stability blocks the escape route and invites perseverance and patience on our part. The means of Benedict's Rule is stability, but the end is that the individual may have space and time for solitude and reflection. There is no room for evasion, for the faces of God in our neighbors and brothers and sisters will not go away. In this way, the stable, unchanging surroundings bring us into a state of reality and true presence. Ultimately the stability of space and relationship — these unchanging mirrors of the soul — are not about geographical space, but spiritual space. They show the unrelenting reflection of our spiritual condition and our heart, our inner cohesion and contentment, as well as our disjointedness and discontent.

Most of us end up moving every few years on account of work. There is this better job, a more promising and fulfilling life, and higher pay perhaps. Sometimes we are eager to just get away from a difficult work situation that felt alienating or abusive; other times, there is the lure and the promise of self-fulfillment through enhanced work opportunities and the status that comes with it. Each move, each job change brings an avalanche of outward newness and unfamiliar sites. As a result, our energies focus on getting ourselves acclimated, showing our colleagues and superiors what we are about, establishing our worth by the work we do. We are oriented toward the outside world with every move we make. Stability, on the other hand, has to do with exploring and finding the internal space each of us carries within. This type of exploration is entirely undramatic. It does not distract and dazzle us by its newness, as does traveling, changing work assignments, making new acquaintances, scoring successes aimed at public recognition. Staying put, repeatedly doing the same job, keeping and renewing largely the same circle of friends, regarding success as simply having done what we were called on to do — keeps us "in place," while laying bare vistas that transcend outer space and time.

Staying put and in place is uncomfortable and disquieting. It means sticking things out in the situation in which God has put us and in the context of the people we find there. But it also creates in us the recognition that our self-worth is not defined by our work. The one doing the same type of work, year in year out, may be closer to the truth than the one forever looking outside of self for fulfillment. According to philosopher Diogenes Allen, "labor by its monotony, by its repetition, by its boredom can teach us what it is to be a human being without God. It can teach us that we are hungry for something more than we have, hungry for more than anything the world has or can give."[8]

Stability is also about the willingness to persevere, to live with the discomfort, and to wait and see what happens after the discomfort subsides. The poet Emily Dickinson once said, "After great pain, a formal feeling comes — The Nerves sit ceremonious, like Tombs."[9] Most of us would rather sedate the pain than endure it and wait for our nerves to settle. But doing so shortchanges the outcome. For after the long, uncomfortable stretch that requires patience and involves suffering, there comes the resolution: accepting ourselves and learning to know who we are. It is the moment of "letting go" and saying "yes" to self.

Enduring the series of crises and tests without bowing out takes us to the cross and its mystery. We are being "put to death continually; we are regarded as sheep marked for slaughter," says Benedict in quoting the Apostle Paul (C 7:38; Rom. 8:36). The goal is not to get by unscathed and unhurt, but to hold on against all odds, placing ourselves at the foot of the cross. It is there that the "formal feeling" comes, where we have given up and surrendered ourselves to death with Christ, and where the stage is set for a resurrected life. Stability—the place of no escape—helps us die, over and over again, in the loneliness and distress felt in the solitary spaces of the heart. We cannot know the peace, the wholeness, the new life in Christ, unless we have sat through the pain and given it sufficient time to transform us.

Popular opinion has it that the monastery is hardly the place to understand the world God created. Why would we need a monastic rule and a place of separation and solitude to become better connected with the world and God? Joan Chittister puts it very simply: "It may be only from a distance that we can see best." Perhaps it is those without money "who best know that money is not essential to the good life. It may be those who each have only a bed and books and one closetful of clothes in one small room to call their own who can clearly realize what clutter can do to a life. It may be those who vow obedience to another who can sense what self-centeredness can do to corrode the heart. It may be only those who stand alone in life who can really know what community is all about."[10] Thus, monastics, by their pronounced and bold practice of the solitary life in a community committed to stability can teach us about the call of every Christian: to step back and reevaluate our priorities, loyalties, and attachments.

Distancing ourselves from the world in order to understand it is frightening. And it takes patience. The novice, or the one inquiring to join the monastic community, is given several hurdles to climb. "Do not grant newcomers to the monastic life an easy entry," Benedict had written in his Rule. Then the novice is warned about the hardships and difficulties that will lie on the way to God (C 58). If the novice promises perseverance in stability after two months, the Rule is read straight through with the words, "This is the law under which you are choosing to serve. If you can keep it, come in. If not, feel free to leave" (C 58). If the novice still stands firm, he is taken back into the novitiate and tested again after six months and then again four months later. Each time the phrase "if he still stands firm" is used. Only then can the novice gain entrance to the community, and his promise in form of a written and signed document is solemnly placed on the altar. The process of gaining entry into the community takes patience and the willingness to persevere.

The repeated testing and the reminder to stand firm are reminiscent of the exodus account. Moses urged the Israelites at the crossing of the Red Sea to fear not, stand firm, and keep their mouths shut. They wavered, for they feared for their lives, they faltered in their promises, and they repeatedly grumbled. In light of Moses' and Benedict's recommendations, the advice for those of us seeking a deeper and more intimate walk with God might be: don't be afraid of solitude; persevere in its frightening, disheartening moments; and stop grumbling and complaining.

Three

The Practices of Solitude

14

Starting with the Questions

What are the ways and tools to help us separate and detach from what we know to be a potential stumbling block, an idol, and an obstacle between us and God? Before we can discern how to better connect with God, we need to ask ourselves some questions: Do we believe that the ties with others, the things we cherish, are ties that blind and bind? Or are we inclined to see that which binds as a means of grounding us in our immediate environment, a vehicle to move us from Point A to Point B, with plenty of leeway to the left and right to find our way back to God? Cutting a pathway through the brambles and weeds of self-deception will mean asking ourselves these questions. The poet Rainer Maria Rilke initially disappointed a young admirer who had sent him his poetry for feedback and who was eager to learn Rilke's tricks of the trade. What are the rules, what are the practices of writing, Franz Xaver Kappus had asked in his letters to the master.

During a correspondence spanning about two years, Rilke instructed his young friend not on the practical means of writing, the do's and don'ts of the craft, but the process of positioning oneself in the way of questions and finding one's own truths in time. "Allow your answers their own solitary undisturbed maturing, which, like any form of progress, has to come from deep within and which cannot be pushed or accelerated. Everything is to be carried full term before it can be born." Insight, Rilke told Kappus, "only comes to those who wait. I myself learn it daily, amidst much pain, for which I am grateful: patience is everything!"[1]

Rilke advised Kappus to stick with what was contained in nature — the simple, the small, the hardly noticeable — and to become its servant. For then, "everything will grow lighter and more unified and somewhat more conciliatory, not in the intellect perhaps, which lags behind in surprise, but in your innermost awareness, your waking moments and your knowing." Therefore, "I beg of you to have patience with all unresolved issues in your heart and to try to love the questions themselves like locked-up rooms and like books written in a very strange tongue. Do not at this point probe after answers, which cannot be given you because you do not have the capacity to live them. The issue is to live out everything. At this point in time live the questions. Perhaps you will then one day, without even noticing, live into the answers."[2]

Our task is to ask questions that fit our height and weight, questions also that are not bigger than life but come in bite-size format. No one can answer for me or offer a one-size-fits-all tool that will magically fix everything. The question for me — at this point in my career, in my journey, in my interconnectedness with others—will be a gauge, a barometer of my internal state. Rather than being a springboard toward resolution and a defined end, it is a tool to measure my state of awareness, my being awake to the blinding and binding ties, inviting utter honesty to myself and to the God who made me. No one has to know how I am doing with the answers, or whether I am finding any answers at all. What I am concerned with is opening myself up to see and understand what has driven me and what has kept me asleep.

Four areas are of particular interest in this process of questioning: (1) What I do and why I do what I do; (2) what about others annoys or distresses me; (3) what thoughts and feelings, praise and criticism, I revisit over and over; and (4) what gratifications my body craves? Stepping back to dwell on these questions without seeking quick answers is important. Answers may form a temporary bridge away from our tension, dismay, and loneliness. Leaning into the questions keeps us focused. "Love your solitude," Rilke advised, "and carry the pain it has caused you with a harmonious-sounding elegy. For those that are near you, are in reality far away, you say, and that shows that it is beginning to grow wide around you. And when your closeness diminishes, then your vastness has reached the stars and is big; rejoice in this your growth, into which you cannot take anybody else with you."[3]

When experiencing this vastness that reaches near the stars, the temptation we face is spiritual pride. After hours of immersing myself in the reading of theology, philosophy, poetry, my mind is carried into a sphere that makes domestic concerns, for example, look trifling and mundane. I am reminded of the Gospel story where Jesus visits the sisters Martha and Mary: one slaves in the kitchen with sweat dripping off her brow and strands of hair coming loose, the other sits in perfect comfort and far away from the scorching fire pit and the kettle fumes to listen to Jesus (Luke 10:38–42). It is tempting to devalue the domestic for the sake of deep thought. It is also tempting to display one's superiority gained through quiet reflection and to seek to bring others along. "Be good toward those who lag behind," says Rilke, "and be firm and calm around them and do not torture them with your doubts, nor frighten them with your certitude or joy, which they cannot comprehend. It is better to look for some simple and steady commonality between you and them, which does not have to change even if you do.... Be compassionate toward those growing older and fearful of solitude, while you have placed your trust in it."[4]

A first step in creating a solitary space and a place for God is to open ourselves to our sacred questions: the questions of our attachments and ties, our passions and dislikes, and the immediate and practical claims placed on us by our environment. For the Christian, corporate worship provides the weekly context for this encounter. Karl Barth, the Swiss Reformed theologian, said that people come to worship with one question on their mind: "Is it true?" Is the God you are telling me about the same God who is seeking me and desirous of my attention and intimate communion? Is there a God vacuum inside my soul that only God can fill but which I have filled with weak and unsatisfying substitutes? Public worship means entering into the "God question" with eyes and ears open, expecting that we will encounter the divine presence and its claims on us, and to the question Barth posed—Is it true?—experience a subtle "yes." Holding on to the question tenaciously from beginning of the liturgy to the end, from opening prayer to closing benediction, is not easy. For me, it is tempting to focus on the homiletical skills—or the ineptness—of the preacher, the diction of the liturgist, or the choir director's selection of anthems and hymns.

We may be enticed to jump the church ship altogether or abandon the question when the preaching bores us, when worship draws attention to its leaders instead of God, or when liturgy is uncoordinated and dissatisfying. But we need to remember that even in the midst of the most rugged liturgy, carried out by a company of misguided guides, Christ is present and able to speak.

The consumer mentality is not stopped short at the church doors, but has turned us — church members and

clergy alike — into liturgical customers demanding to be
served the best product money can buy, one that promises
self-improvement with an entertaining touch and possibly
an educational self-help edge. The question "Is it true?"
morphs into "Does it serve me?" or "Is it well done and
fun?" Recovering the right question when entering public
worship and holding on to it well to the end, will be key in
waiting for the divine mystery to unfold in its answer to us.

15

Singing God's Praises
with a Question Mark

Placing ourselves in public worship while setting aside the
customer mentality that rates and evaluates means we
can begin to engage the question "Is it true?" "Show me,
God, that you are alive and interested in making me your
dwelling place!" is the prayer with which to enter the sanctuary. "Allow me to look beyond your fumbling servants —
myself included." Our inner dialogue prior to entering the
sanctuary excuses the faux pas bound to happen. We also
prepare space for the divine presence, silence for the sound
from beyond, and a relatively clean sheet for God to write
on. Certainly some church settings and leaders are better
at creating a worshipful environment than others. But no
matter where we worship, we are invited to open ourselves

to God's movement in our lives and to hear God speaking. Are there places and churches I would rather be? No doubt there are, but I need to remind myself that I am here now and I am willing to lay aside my delimiting mind-set to let in whatever crumbs and rays are strewn my way.

I have known people who have been attending worship for years without seemingly carrying a single question for God. Perhaps it was there once, but they may have long forgotten. They go every Sunday as a sort of penance, or in an effort to become convinced that their intentions toward God are good. The flesh is there; the mind is elsewhere. Thus, public worship has become an anemic ritual, emptied of the expectation of a mystery unveiled, drained of the potential to offer a sight too blinding to bear. Without a single question in mind, it is hard to truly hear something other than the religious-sounding background noise of music and words that produces the illusion of being near God. The inner space has not been prepared. Instead of even a small vacancy for God, the soul is owner-occupied. It is quite possible that well-meaning Christians, intent on outward piety and stellar church activity, have given the rest of us the impression that we are unreasonable, demanding, and impious rebels for asking and expecting to see the Holy revealed in worship.

The revelation of the Holy is certainly not up to us. But perceiving the Holy is. Such perception begins with a pulling back and away from outer connectedness. Though we are in community, involved in the communal worship life, the question we bring to God creates a space that is solitary, a vacuum outlined by uncertainty. This uncertainty hampers the ego from taking the seat reserved for God alone. And by this kind of uncertainty, a type of *askesis* or confinement forms. We voluntarily choose to deprive ourselves of those things that give us a sure footing, a prideful certainty, and a strength derived from self. Every act of public worship should begin with this confinement of self, resulting in an uncontrolled openness to God.

As we enter the sanctuary, we need to take the time to formulate the question we bring. Rather than scanning the pews to see who is there or who is wearing what or whether the scriptures or selected hymns are familiar to us, we might focus on the question we bring to God this day. What causes me distress, what limits my ability to show love and kindness toward others, where have I been defensive and harmed people in word and deed? Formulating our questions is a type of prayer. It is as if we are repeating the words of the Taizé chant: "O Lord, hear my prayer, O Lord, hear my prayer, when I call, answer me." Our sustained attention throughout the worship service in waiting for God's answer is an act of voluntary confinement that leads to a solitary place—a place where we can hear God speak because God's servant is listening.

16

Locking Up the Ego

The confining of our ego, or *askesis,* is a deliberate interference with our god-lust, our presumption to be as gods. We recognize and acknowledge this experience most frequently when it is imposed on us. Difficult as it is to endure, its silver linings can be appreciated only much later. "This was the best thing that ever happened to me," we hear people say when describing the aftermath of a relationship breakup, a personal crisis, a loss. Suddenly, instead of mechanically and obliviously pursuing day-to-day goals and objectives, the person is confronted with a door that's bolted shut. An illness, a job loss, a divorce can force us to stop doing and thinking the way we have grown accustomed to and jolt us awake. A new reality breaks in, one that discloses our human limits. Relentlessly pulled out of self-sufficiency and our godlike illusion of self, we are surprised to enter not a diminished and crippled life, but one that has grown larger and deeper and more concrete.

In *Migrations to Solitude,* Sue Halpern interviews people on a sojourn to solitude, either as a result of their own choosing or by force of outside conditions. She collects the wisdom of solitaries, from the homeless person to the patient in hospice care or living with the HIV/AIDs virus, from secular hermits to Trappist monks, from the prisoner in solitary confinement to the patient in the hospital's intensive care unit.[1] The reader discovers among all of these people's stories a single thread: the state of self-absorption metamorphoses into a growing dependence on the Other; the habitual human connectedness, now severed, transforms into the dawning recognition of the solitary clearing that invites authenticity — being oneself without apologies, a peaceful interconnectedness with all things, and with God.

One frequently overlooked form of involuntary *askesis* is imprisonment. Given the security obstacles created by the state and federal prison system for visitors and non-family members, and the shame and secrecy attached to the status of ex-convict, we may never encounter prisoners in their environment or consciously make the acquaintance of someone previously incarcerated. Those shoved to the

periphery of society and forgotten behind bars give eloquent testimony of solitude's value.

Some of the most compelling insights into Christian discipleship were written in prison. The New Testament provides
us with the so-called captivity letters of the Apostle Paul.[2]
"Devote yourselves to prayer," he writes to the Colossians,
"keeping alert in it with thanksgiving. At the same time pray
for us as well that God will open to us a door for the word,
that we may declare the mystery of Christ, for which I am in
prison, so that I may reveal it clearly as I should" (Col. 4:2–
4). In addition, there is the Book of Revelation, written by
John the Divine, who had spent his life nurturing his seven
parishes (which he may have helped to found) and who was
made to pay for it: "I, John, your brother who share with
you in Jesus the persecution and the kingdom and the patient endurance, was on the island called Patmos because
of the word of God and the testimony of Jesus" (Rev. 1:9),
John writes. He had been exiled to the small island to live
there as a convict among stone quarries.

There are also the letters from prison by John of the Cross
in Toledo, Spain; Dietrich Bonhoeffer in Tegel, near Berlin;
Martin Luther King Jr. in Birmingham; Aleksandr Solzhe-
nitsyn in the Russian gulag. They all give testimony to the
creative energies unleashed by confinement in a cell, and
the deep, heartfelt expression of gratitude that emerges.
"You must know that there is not even an atom of reproach
of bitterness in me about what has befallen the two of us,"
writes Bonhoeffer to his brother-in-law Hans von Dohnanyi
when both are imprisoned for their involvement in a plot to
kill the Nazi dictator Adolf Hitler. For before God "there can
only be subjection, perseverance, patience — in gratitude.
So every question 'Why?' falls silent, because it has found
its answer." Therefore, "what we cannot do," he says, "we
must now simply let go of and limit ourselves to what we

can do and should do, that is be firm and strong in trust in God in the midst of our suffering."[3] The same month that he wrote those words, Bonhoeffer also scribbled on a notepad the phrases "separation from people, from work, from the past, from the future, from marriage, from God," along with such catchphrases as "self-deception, idealizing of the past and of the present; overcoming memories," "the significance of illusion," and wordplays on the meaning and function of time as "an experience of separation" and the "emptiness of time despite all that fills it."[4]

The need to fill the emptiness of time in confinement activates the imagination. The limited resources available prompt their repeated use. And by the repeated use of limited resources, gifts of which one had previously been unaware are discovered and honed. After a year in prison, Bonhoeffer, for example, surprised himself by writing poetry—an art form he would have approved of only when placed in direct service to God's Word, such as in biblical prophesy, the psalms, and hymnody. "Up to now I've been keeping it dark from everyone," he writes coyly to his friend Eberhard Bethge,[5] and "I hope that if need be you will tick me off and tell me clearly not to meddle with it."[6] But Bethge responded with encouragement and Bonhoeffer continued writing. In the poem "Who Am I?" Bonhoeffer gives voice to the emotional upheaval his confinement is causing him. He is "struggling for breath," "yearning for colors," "thirsting for words of kindness," "trembling with anger at despotisms," "tossing in expectation," being "restless and longing and sick, like a bird in a cage."[7] The poem ends on a key of deeply mined wisdom and depth:

Who am I? This or the other?
Am I one person today, and tomorrow another?
Am I both at once? A hypocrite before others,

and before myself a contemptibly woebegone
  weakling?
Or is something within me still like a beaten army,
fleeing in disorder from victory already achieved?

Who am I? They mock me, these lonely questions of
  mine.
Whoever I am, thou knowest, O God, I am thine.[8]

In the confining conditions of prison, the repeated use
of the resources at hand can unearth truths, insights, and
beauty that otherwise would have remained concealed. We,
those on the outside with unlimited freedom and a wealth
of choices, are heirs and beneficiaries of these treasures.
About his eremitic and contemplative life, Thomas Merton wrote to Dom Francis Decroix: "My brother, perhaps
in my solitude I have become as it were an explorer for
you, a searcher in realms which you are not able to visit—
except perhaps in the company of your psychiatrist." In
1997, Anthony Lee Brown, a prisoner convicted of mur-
der and imprisoned for the previous twenty years, wrote
about discovering Merton's writings on solitude: "I was as-
tonished when I read those words for the first time nearly
a decade ago. Feeling a kinship difficult to describe, but
possibly comparable to that shared by the hijacked, kid-
napped, or shipwrecked, I saw in those words the thoughts
of a man willingly wandering a landscape that had been
my terror and home for many years. Although not a voluntary explorer, and certainly never a monk, nor even much
of a human being, but, instead, a convicted murderer and
thief trying to remain sane and understand the purpose of
his existence, I knew well the place my brother spoke of—
a dark and frightening nightmare domain, spiritual and
corporeal, strange and illogical, barren and violent, peo-

pled by twisting specters of shredded human souls, and illuminated by the burning oils of their crushed spirits...the penitentiary."[9]

Brown, writing from the Spring Creek Correctional Facility in Seward, Alaska, continued: "Somewhat like a monk insulated from the world by monastery walls, a prisoner-penitent sequestered from life beyond the walls, fences, and razor wire of his cage may have the opportunity to develop a perspective that is both unique to one's circumstance and, perhaps, otherwise unattainable. My experience has taught me that given longevity, survival, and sanity this perspective can be advantageous and of practical benefit. An example of the fruit of this perspective is my understanding of the cultivation of my character in light of my family dynamic, which in turn has helped me to change my behaviors, nurture the growth of spiritual characteristics, and encourage similar insight and change in others."[10] In Brown's case, the high-powered compression and violent shock waves of imprisonment and isolation had churned out a diamond, which by its sheer luminescence dazzles and draws. We benefit from the insights of those subject to forced solitude and confining conditions. And by their writings and reflections we are emboldened to find our own solitary space before God.

Shortly after my conversion experience, I came across the writings of St. Teresa of Avila and her collaborator St. John of the Cross. I was enthralled by Teresa's visions of the soul as an "interior castle" and John's meditations on descent into "the dark night of the soul" prior to ascent and union with God. Little did I know at the time that Teresa was scrupulously enclosed within the walls of her order's convent. Later she would establish sixteen Carmelite convents designed for those wishing to develop greater spiritual depth by living under more austere, restricted, and confined conditions than were the custom in either Spain or Italy at the time. Neither was I aware that John had written *The Dark Night* along with his *Living Flame of Love* while in a Toledo prison. Perhaps it was the luminescence of a diamond I had glimpsed in their writings. And perhaps it was this sparkle that should later draw me to become involved in prison and jail ministry, first by being a pen pal to prison inmates as part of Chuck Colson's national ministry, Prison Fellowship, and later by jump-starting jail ministries at several of the churches I served.

For years, a number of our church members would coordinate biweekly or monthly worship services in the local county jail, leading groups of male or female inmates in hymn singing and prayer, providing meditations on the scriptures and giving personal testimonies, and taking back to our congregation the inmates' written prayer requests. In the beginning, I am fairly sure that most of us had no idea what we were supposed to be doing, let alone why we were doing it. We simply wanted to be faithful Christians and we believed faithfulness—no matter how inadequately realized—involved doing works of mercy extended to "one of the least of these" in Christ's family, the inmates at our county jail. Then one day, following worship, the question was set before us plainly. "Whatcha doin' here anyways?" one of the inmates demanded to know. "Wa's in it for you!" His defiant scowl and the measured trace of hostility in his voice didn't escape us and our eyes darted to the chapel door, which, for security reasons—whose security?—the guards had bolted shut from the outside. "Yeah, wa's in it for you!" repeated a chorus of husky voices from the back. As the team's leader I felt provoked to defend the purity of our motives, while regarding it as a prime teaching moment to elaborate on the Christian principle of self-giving love. Luckily I kept my mouth shut. While the other team members were fielding the question with a profusion of kindnesses ("We love you; we want you to know the love of Jesus"), something dawned on me. These inmates—representing both the sophisticated and the uncouth, the soft-spoken and the loud, the devious and the devout—had one thing in common: they were wide awake to the proclamation of God's word, reaching for it, squeezing it, and knocking it around like a basketball. The gleam in their eyes when singing or listening, the tears rolling down unconcealed, proved *me* guilty: guilty of apathy, of taking for granted my ample freedom, of taking for granted God. By the time hardly anybody was listening, I said, "We are here because you have something we've forgotten all about."

The purpose of locking up and confining our ego is to wake us up so we can remember what we've forgotten. To place ourselves into an ascetic environment is like volunteering to enter a cell, a place of confinement, a space that has boundaries and walls. It is no coincidence that monastic dwellings in the desert and in monasteries or convents are called cells. Not unlike prison cells, they confine each resident to a small, restricted area in which to do battle with the forces of passion, emotion, and motive. Cells in themselves do not produce a deepened and more authentic life, but they do set up the conditions, prepare the soil that makes such a life possible, and enable the seedlings of wisdom to grow.

How then can we, those not imprisoned nor living as monastics and recluses, create the outer conditions of confinement that will connect us more deeply with God within? When looking at some of the ascetic practices, a word of caution is in order. Eugene Peterson puts it succinctly: "The basic necessity for and nature of *askesis* has been badly obscured in our time by chatty devotionalism and the hawking of 'spiritual disciplines,' as if spirituality were a mood that we can self-induce and spiritual disciplines were techniques that we can put to use to tend to the well-being of our souls." With the consumer mentality a common mindset, we "must begin by insisting that *askesis* is not a spiritual technology at our beck and call but is rather immersion in an environment in which our capacities are reduced to nothing, or nearly nothing and we are at the mercy of God to shape his will in us."[11] Reading about the spiritual disciplines is like reading about exercise without doing it, about prayer without pausing to bow our head, about a foreign language without putting its odd-shaped vocabulary on our tongue and to the test. Spiritual disciplines need repeated application. As ordering principles and imaginary walls of confinement, they can put us into a learning and discovery mode regarding the spiritual landscape. From the wide range of spiritual disciplines, I have chosen a sample. The purpose is not to be comprehensive (Richard Foster and Dallas Willard have done that already for us, among others), but to generate comprehension and to illustrate how a particular discipline can assist us in preparing a space for God. For reasons of clarity, I have grouped them into roughly three categories: mixed disciplines engaging simultaneously both body and soul; disciplines directed primarily at the body; and disciplines directed primarily at the soul.

Body and Soul on the Treadmill

Our church has a group that meets on Monday mornings for exercise. Since my office is right down the hall, I hear the music resounding, and through the glass doors I can see the shadows of bodies swaying as one to the rhythm. Sometimes the instructor's voice intones the next movement above the music; other times I hear members praying and humming while their bodies keep moving to give expression to what they hear and hum. The name of the group is Body and Soul—a fortuitous descriptor of the group's activity and a metaphor of the spiritual disciplines involving both our body and soul, prodding us at once to get unstuck and become more nimble, flexible, and responsive to the rhythm and heartbeat of God.

Corporate worship is, or could be, like that. We stand for the opening hymn, sit for the confession, stand for the Gospel proclamation, sit for the exposition of scripture, and stand again for the charge and benediction as a sign of our readiness to go into the world to carry out Christ's great commission. Alternating between postures in synchronicity with what is heard is a body-and-soul exercise. Anyone who has "sat" through a worship service at an African American church has done very little sitting, but rather has stood, swayed, stomped, clapped, crossed the sanctuary during the passing of the peace, hugged much, and marched to the front of the church during the offertory or communion. Body and soul are warmed up by stretching exercises, tight vocal cords and fists are loosened, and stiff necks and hearts are musically and soulfully massaged and rhythmically unwound. Pentecostal and charismatic Christian traditions employ a similarly engaging liturgy that attempts to synchronize body and soul, allowing for physical expressions of the fullness of the heart.

ATTENDING WORSHIP

Traces of this synchronicity exist in most mainline liturgical traditions. The most common and perhaps least acknowledged trace is the expectation that followers of Christ regularly attend church on the Sabbath day. "I had my church on television" is a frequent comment I hear from members who skipped church. While the soul may have been fed, the body remains largely uninvolved, for the physical effort of getting up, getting dressed, and taking myself into the crowd of others has been eschewed. According to pastor and theologian Brian McLaren, spiritual disciplines, including worship attendance, aim at spiritual formation. They are actions within our power to help us become people we are currently incapable of being. Attending worship is a spiritual discipline involving body and soul that bears the marks of "inconvenience, association, and speed."[1] By making myself go to church, I am inconvenienced by going to a place I didn't choose, at a time I didn't choose, for a purpose I choose. By my physical presence among other worshipers, I come to associate with some people I like, with others I don't like, for a purpose I believe in. And by placing myself in an environment with a certain liturgy aimed at allowing me to encounter God, I change my day-to-day speed, altering my pace to discover what I may have overlooked and to feel a different rhythm. Behind the dictum that one "ought to go" to church lies less a divine command to conform to religious tradition than the validation of a spiritual discipline's effectiveness. We do it not because it is religious law, but because it is an action within our power to become people we are currently incapable of being.

So how does our worship attendance provide a solitary space? Would not staying at home by ourselves, worshiping with the television or religious radio broadcast, hold greater promise of solitude? To put it simply, virtual electronic reality cannot substitute for being in the presence of our brothers and sisters in Christ. It takes a visit onsite to experience the messiness of human vehicles acting as divine messengers and unpredictable, yet irreversibly appointed, members of Christ's body. You have to sit in the pew to feel your back hair rise as your neighbor, undisturbed by and oblivious to the ethereal beauty of the choir's anthem, noisily unwraps a cough drop. You have to feel the sticky palms of the two-year-old grabbing and wrapping around your legs like an octopus. You have to overhear the giddy whispers of approval and see the enraptured facial expressions of members over a sermon during which God most certainly left the room.

To experience physicality and divinity meeting in the place of worship mirrors who we are: it reflects back to us our impatience with our physicality, our incipient urge to control what we cannot, and the courage of God to become flesh even and especially in us. Recognizing our lack of patience and forgiveness, and our gratitude for God's patience with us and forgiveness toward us are gifts we take away from public worship. Perhaps at worship we also catch a glimpse of that which unites us all — the spiritual community birthed by Christ in ragtag human vessels, invited to become aware of where we need to change and decrease — in our actions, thoughts, and desires — so God may increase.

SACRAMENTS

The sacraments in worship are actions of our body and soul that prepare us for a solitary encounter with God. Here the elements of water, bread, and wine touch and enter our bodies. The exodus experience of the Israelites is reenacted by water, bread, drink. In the worship service at our church, the baptismal font is the focal point, placed in front of the communion table. It always is filled with water as a symbol of our own baptism, the sign and seal that marks us as Christ's own. Early on in the liturgy we point to this invisible mark during our confession and assurance of pardon. "Remember your baptism," the minister says, "and know that you are forgiven."

How do we remember our baptism when we were infants, as most of us were at the time of baptism, half asleep or screaming in our mother's arms? We do it by imagination. We relive the act and its meaning. We embrace the mark of liberation that has made us members of a community that lives in heaven and on earth with Christ as head. See the waters of baptism forming a pathway through the Red Sea. See the turbulent waters of this world with all their threatening force. Don't run from them, but place yourself in their way and keep on walking. For it is the walk, your particular walk, with the spray of drops and splashes all over your face and body that marks you as God's elect, as a child of the promise en route to the Promised Land. To remember our baptism means we take initiative through an act of the imagination. Like Jesus we walk the lonesome valley by ourselves. The African American spiritual puts it like this:

> We must walk this lonesome valley,
> we have to walk it by ourselves;
> O, nobody else can walk it for us,
> we have to walk it by ourselves.

And while confronted with the watery wall and the enemies in hot pursuit, we hear the words of Moses as if spoken to us: Fear not, embrace the present situation, and be still without grumbling—so you may hear God speak.

The Eucharist, or Holy Communion, is an extension of the exodus, that solitary sojourn through the Red Sea into wilderness territory and on toward the Promised Land. The Israelites passed through the Red Sea only once, but they were fed repeatedly. They gathered the manna off the ground and drank of water bubbling from rock. They were to eat and drink only what they needed. Nothing was to be stored, put aside, or carried back and given to someone else. In our communion service, we have plates of bread and trays of grape juice that are passed from one end of the pew to the other. We sit, take what is passed, and eat and drink what we hold in our hand. It is a convenient and efficient way of distributing the bread and the cup, but from a theological perspective not the most telling or dramatic. After all, the scriptures read and proclaimed function as an altar call of sorts. As God's Word they call us to respond, using our free will: the taking or leaving of it, the eating or refusing to eat and drink Christ's body and blood. Taking implies initiative, and what better way to take initiative than responding in physical movement: getting up on our feet, filing out of the pew, standing in line, walking toward the cross until it is our turn to receive into our hands and feel on our lips what Christ has prepared.

The bulletin of a Presbyterian church in Cincinnati explains why their worshiping community alternates between the two modes of partaking of the Eucharist: "Serving in the pews emphasizes the communal nature of the sacrament — we partake together. Coming forward for communion by intinction emphasizes the individual's relationship to God — each is served individually."[2] Intentionally moving our bodies toward the place of nourishment, standing so everyone still in their seats can see us, and holding out our hand for food and drink is a solitary act — as is eating and drinking, receiving for our own body and our own soul the body Christ gave, the blood Christ shed. "The body of Christ broken for you" invites us to break away from what binds and motivates us to become as a god, and instead to make room for the true God. "The blood of Christ shed for you" calls us to stop denying and running from our pain and brokenness and instead acknowledge it and then surrender to the new life of Christ within.

SECRET WORKS OF MERCY

In the Sermon on the Mount, Jesus commended to us the works of mercy, such as giving alms to the poor, visiting the sick and those in prison, feeding and clothing the hungry and destitute. In our churches, the mercy workers are often those ordained as deacons or those passionate about local and global mission, serving in soup kitchens, building homes for the poor, tutoring children in the inner city. The compartmentalizing of Christians into mercy workers and those who fill other ministry functions has obscured the call extended to all Christians to be engaged in the building up of the body of Christ. The leaders of the eighteenth-century movement called Methodism give ample witness to this principle.

John Wesley believed that Jesus Christ is "God's chief means of grace," but from our end we are asked to contribute the means of grace through our "works of piety" (spiritual disciplines) and "works of mercy" (doing good for others). The spiritual discipline involved in doing works of mercy is discreteness and secrecy. In commenting on almsgiving in Jesus' Sermon on the Mount, Wesley says: "And, First, with regard to works of mercy. 'Take heed,' saith he, 'that ye do not your alms before men, to be seen of them: Otherwise ye have no reward of your Father which is in heaven.' "[3]

This discreteness is not limited to almsgiving but applies to every work of charity. "Every thing which we give, or speak, or do, whereby our neighbour may be profited; whereby another man may receive any advantage, either in his body or soul" is to be done not for communal approval but for the singular approval of God. "The feeding the hungry, the clothing the naked, the entertaining or assisting the stranger, the visiting those that are sick or in prison, the comforting the afflicted, the instructing the ignorant, the reproving the wicked, the exhorting and encouraging the well-doer; and if there be any other work of mercy, it is equally included in this direction," Wesley says.[4] Though these acts are largely done in community and for the benefit of the greater community, we serve out of an individual, solitary conviction and we play to an audience of One. Practicing discreteness in the good we do in service to Christ is aimed at creating intentional solitude.

SPIRITUAL FRIENDS AND SPIRITUAL DIRECTION

The Methodist movement began when George Whitfield (1714–70), an Anglican priest, invited Anglican priests John and Charles Wesley to join him in preaching the Gospel where it was most needed: not from church pulpits

but on the streets and in the fields of the common labor-
ers and the unchurched. Later, the Wesleys organized the
new converts into small groups called bands, classes, and
societies. In these groups, people helped one another experience transformation, so that within weeks, months,
and years there were thousands of people whose lives were
transformed by the works of mercy and piety. According to
Brian McLaren, it was like "a group of people ascending a
mountain, each one always having someone a step above
and ahead of them to emulate and follow, plus someone
a step behind and below to encourage and bring upward
and onward."[5] Not until the Wesleys, says McLaren, "did
anyone do for spiritual formation what Luther and Calvin
had done for doctrine: create a system to replace what had
been rejected from Catholicism."[6]

Today the search for means of spiritual transformation
has taken us back to contemplative practices and medieval
monastic disciplines. It has also taken us to revisit Wesleyan
Methodism with its emphasis on small groups and spiritual
friends. This new type of "methodism" aimed at spiritual
transformation will see, in McLaren's words, "discipleship
as the process of reaching ahead with one hand to find the
hand of a mentor a few steps up the hill, while reaching
back with the other to help the next brother or sister in line
who is also on the upward path of discipleship."[7]

For me, finding the hand of a mentor whom I could respect and trust has been no small task. Over the years, I
have found such mentors, or spiritual directors, mostly by
word of mouth. Catholic and Episcopal priests, as well as
monastics and members of religious orders, are expected to
be in spiritual direction. They naturally know who is available and trained at the task. Mentor and mentee will need
rapport, preferring to think and speak along the same or
similar lines of reasoning and perceiving, and being open

to periodically evaluating the relationship to determine if each is still clasping the hand of the other during the ascent. All my spiritual directors have been women (by choice) and most were monastics (by chance). Their lives were filled with prayer, contemplation, and works of mercy, and through them I could see Christ gently inviting me to lay bare my soul. "How are things with your soul?" my current spiritual director, an I.H.M. sister and retired superintendent of public schools, asks me at the beginning of each monthly meeting. And then it's my turn to unload — the beautiful, the mediocre, and the ugly.

In spiritual direction, we intentionally put both body and soul at the mercy of another. At least once a month, I become a conscientious mercy recipient, someone who admits to standing in need of correction, instruction, and mirroring for my soul. According to Margaret Guenther, spiritual direction is "holy listening" on the part of the director and a form of holy searching on the part of the one directed. "Good Teacher, what must I do to inherit eternal life?" (Mark 10:17) is the central question of the one seeking direction, though he or she may not be aware of it.[8] This question is reiterated in the sayings of the desert fathers and mothers, where the disciple or seeker inquires of the spiritual teacher about a word from the Lord and the way to salvation. A disciple asked Abba Antony, "What shall I do?" And the old man answered, "Don't be confident in your own righteousness; don't grieve over a thing that is past; and be chaste with your tongue and your belly."[9]

As in the relationship between disciple and *abba* or *amma*, the account of the rich young man approaching Jesus for guidance implies a hierarchical relationship and an affectionate connection based on love. This hierarchy is "a gentle and perhaps transitory one," says Guenther, where the teacher provides the context for the disciple to make new discoveries and gain fresh insights. At the same time, "the questioner must be free to deal with and even learn to love the question."[10] Implied in spiritual direction are two attitudes that run counter to what we perceive as essential Christian virtues: caring and knowing. According to Eugene Peterson, spiritual direction is just the opposite: it's the practice of intentionally detaching from knowledge and compassion, so as to become "unknowing" and "uncaring."[11] As spiritual mentors one to another, we are called on to do what does not come easily in a goal-oriented, information-filled, and activity-driven culture: the practice of stepping back from assuming that we know and have something to teach and yielding to mystery as it unfolds in the encounter; and the practice of guarding against the impulse to be helpful so as to allow the Spirit to do its work.

In the relationship with my spiritual director, I am the one who lags multiple steps behind. It is exhilarating, instructive, and motivating to have a mentor who is eloquent, intelligent, and deeply immersed in religious life. But it is difficult as well. I admit that there have been times when I wanted to run or cut short our meetings because what I saw in myself wasn't pleasant to behold. There have been times when I expected praise and affirmation and none came, other times when I was commended for the progress I had made without having a clue that I'd been making any. Spiritual direction is a little bit like the monthly massage I get. I undress and lie naked on the table to let the massage therapist feel out and undo the twisted and tensed muscles before they cause me severe pain. While I'm lying there, exposed to her relentless hands kneading away, I try to endure the discomfort. But I stay, not because I enjoy feeling like a lamb bound and served up on the altar, but because experience tells me that the temporary discomfort of submission, vulnerability, and exposure brings me long-term relief.

18

Body Guards

In Christian thought, the body is the interface between the world and God. In the body of Jesus, God became flesh to show those living in bodies the nature and likeness of God. Spiritual disciplines help us care for our bodies by causing us to be mindful of what goes in our bodies, whose company we keep, and with what (or with whom) we unite. In responding to questions from the Corinthian church about sexual intercourse, the Apostle Paul retorts, "Do you not know that your bodies are members of Christ?" and "do you not know that your body is a temple of the Holy Spirit within you, which you have from God, and that you are not your own?" (1 Cor. 6:15a, 19). And, finally, "for you were bought with a price; therefore glorify God in your body" (v. 20).

WHAT GOES IN

The medical profession has helped us recognize the impact of diet on our physical well-being. We watch the intake of foods containing saturated fats, cholesterol, sugar, starches, and bleach. But we are less discerning about the literary and electronic company we keep. According to a *Newhouse News* article, "there is a price to pay for living in a world where the news never stops." People bathe in constant news reports "not so much for information as by an addiction to technology and impulses that turn human attention to fear, sex, and conflict." The result is that our minds get filled "with static, distortion and exaggerated anxiety," leading to psychological problems, cynicism, and disengagement and disposing us to "overestimate the amount of violence and bad deeds in the world."[1]

Being aware how much time we spend imbibing news, when and where, along with registering how we feel after "the meal," will help us create a rule of measured intake, a restricted diet, and temporary abstinence. I still vividly recall, years ago, my sense of agitation and outrage on Sunday nights after watching *60 Minutes*. At the time, I was teaching college courses in ethics and journalism, so I felt under a certain professional obligation to keep up with the news and a variety of social ills. But, truth be told, I was no longer the one doing the keeping. The news was "keeping me" and was beginning to shape my view of the world and people in less than positive ways. Add to that the ammunition of theological vocabulary provided by my seminary education, and I was now able to couch the world's evils in theological terms: sin in its complexity, both individual and corporate, lurked everywhere, and I had become its vigilant detector, expositor, and foe. Then one day I caught a glimpse of myself. I don't know whether it was a student, a colleague, or a friend who served as this gracious mirror. All I remember were the consequences: I donated my television set to Goodwill and let my newspaper subscriptions expire as a trade-off for recovering my inner peace.

THE COMPANY WE KEEP

What is true about the news to which we expose ourselves is also true of the people whose company we keep: some infect us with anxiety, cynicism, and unrest, and others provide us with a sense of balance, creativity, and contentment.

How do I discern who is good for me and who is not? Under-lying this question is our search for our true self in God. This search will have to distinguish between the ego that seeks identity by association and the true self that draws identity from belonging to God in Christ. Are we using the friends and acquaintances whose company we seek to boost our ego? Or are we seeking them out for the hand they can lend us in the ascent, for the way they function as a spiritual mentor and role model, for someone to emulate and from whom to learn?

Discerning our motives for friendship will help us identify which relationships to initiate, enhance, or discard. It will also drive us back to solitude, where we see ourselves stretching out one hand to the one leading us upward, the other to the person hanging on to ours. In church we may be singing "What a friend we have in Jesus, all our sins and griefs to bear! What a privilege to carry everything to God in prayer!" but we fail to apply the hymn's wisdom by taking instead all or most of our griefs to those we call friends. Prone to seeking out those who "understand" our grudges and discontent, we call them friends because they often share our own impatience, filling our loneliness by entertaining and distracting chatter, reassuring us of our innocence, and allowing us to remain unchanged. Prayer and solitude are often an afterthought on our list of things to do in times of crisis. In our frantic search of finding "a friend" who will listen, we close the door on the designated Number One friend we have in Christ.

The English language has turned the notion of friend-ship into a generic platitude. We call people "friends" if we once had lunch or dinner with them, know their cell phone number, or correspond with them on occasion by e-mail. The off-handed use of the term "friend" blurs the quality and depth of the relationship and gives the impression that we are connected and not alone, when mostly the opposite is true. Realistically assessing our aloneness, our separateness, and embracing it as a friend, not foe, will take us back to Christ, the source of all connectedness. We can see better from a distance. Distancing allows us to differentiate between our role of mentor or mentee in relation to others, our veiled expectations, and our responsibilities.

We all know people with a "toxic personality." The toxins are less potent when we realize the role we play. If we expect them to guide us along the spiritual journey, we have made a poor choice; if we think we can reach out to them and bring them along by administering a cure, we had better put on protective coveralls and keep our role clearly before us. Much energy is wasted by relationships that are not moving either one of us ahead on the spiritual front. Such relationships keep us stuck to each other as if the hand-holding itself were the goal, not the upward climb. The warm, fuzzy feeling of connectedness has substituted for the gritty growth. Like insurance plans, friendships ought to be reviewed on occasion for the premiums we are charged and the coverage we get. Basing connectedness on the sentimental recollection of a profitable shared past means we are projecting the past into the future and uploading it with unreasonably high promises and hopes. Fostering and maintaining friendship has been an important spiritual practice to me. I like its regularity and ritual, the taking stock, the checking in, the give-and-take, and the dynamics of the alternating role of mentee or mentor. But I admit to having carried on some friendships far too long. Like the daily news, they took over my emotional state, leaving me feeling tense and unbalanced. As a mentor of mine has reminded me on occasion, "You cannot afford them — the premium is too high."

WITH WHAT WE UNITE

The Apostle Paul had sought to impress upon the Christians in Corinth the primordial union that was theirs. "Anyone united to the Lord becomes one spirit with him." Out of this spiritual union springs the cautionary command concerning physical union: "Shun fornication! Every sin that a person commits is outside the body; but the fornicator sins against the body itself" (1 Cor. 6:17–18). I attended church for years, usually two and three times a week, before I heard the word "fornication" spoken or, more accurately, whispered. I knew what "abomination" and "desolation" and "damnation" meant, or thought I did. The whisper indicated to me that "fornication" was something equally dreadful, a member of the dark vocabulary of sin. Indeed, the word's Latin root *fornix* denotes one of the numerous arched underground dwellings in Rome where poor people and prostitutes lived. By definition, fornication is sexual intercourse between a man and a woman outside of marriage.

The word's archaic ring could suggest that the activity is a thing of the past (which, of course, it is not) or that, given the rarity of the word's use in public and private conversations, it is no longer considered an immoral activity to be avoided by followers of Christ. Unlike adultery, which is euphemistically referred to as "having an extramarital affair" (as if it were a shady business deal or cheating on your tax return), fornication has not managed to produce its linguistically updated, modern-day counterpart. While the expression "having premarital sex" describes an activity, it is value neutral, drained of moral judgment. Conversely, to speak of and endorse celibacy—a commitment to sexual abstinence in singleness—frequently unleashes an avalanche of implicit judgment (expressed in mirth and gales of laughter, cynicism, and veiled contempt) even among committed Christians. It is as if popular culture and mores define and evaluate Christian behavior rather than the ordering principles of God, who speaks to his people through the laws of the Old Testament, the prophets, and, most prominently, the person of Jesus Christ and his body, the church.

CELIBATE PRACTICE

Guarding the body against illicit sexual unions is the role of the spiritual discipline of celibacy. For single people, this means a guard, or personal rule, against premarital sex, for married people against extramarital sex. In my own denomination, the Presbyterian Church (USA), this moral tenet is constitutionally anchored and called the "chastity and fidelity clause." It requires that the church's ordained officers—deacons, elders, and ministers of Word and Sacrament — practice celibacy (though the word "chastity" is used) in singleness and fidelity in marriage. While the clause has been hotly debated since its adoption in 1997, attention focuses primarily on two groups: church officers and those in same-sex unions. As the ordering principle for sexual intercourse commended to all Christians becomes blurred, the other church members appear to be off the hook.

In a turn of irony, a celibacy movement has emerged during the last decade not from within the church but out of secular, popular culture. The movement is variously called "Second Virginity" or "The Cult of the Born-Again Virgin" and promotes the temporary and long-term benefits of sexual abstinence. With the motto that "celibacy is sexy," the trend recommends "using abstinence for recharging your spirit, discovering your passions, and achieving greater intimacy in your next relationship."[2] The movement has appealed to women, in particular, who view abstinence as a way of saving themselves for a "higher-quality man." Or, they opt for the practice of a "reclaimed virginity" to create inner peace and balance, attain a higher level of self-actualization, return to core values, or explore more deeply their spirituality. Some want to make more free time, or more money; others start a charity with their newfound strength and purpose, while still others wish "to get in touch with their creative selves, to gather up energy for a life transition, to heal from losses."[3] Books that glorify the benefits of celibacy tend to be peppered with self-help advice: avoid a certain type of partner, embrace your sexual bill of rights, make lists about what you want for yourself and keep them as handy reminders in your purse. Above all, the goal is "to get what you want" and to exert enough will power to bring about the desired outcome—autonomy, sexual independence, and an actualized self.

Another movement is the wave of "chastity chic," spearheaded by celebrities who are publicly confessing to their virginal vows until marriage. Among them are a host of outspoken virgins, such as actresses Jessica Simpson and Lisa Kudrow (Phoebe in the TV sitcom *Friends*) and a member of the Los Angeles Lakers, A. C. Green. Green's virginity is said to have ended at age thirty-eight when he, a devout Christian, married; Simpson, a Baptist minister's daughter who received a chastity ring from her dad at age twelve, was twenty-two and Kudrow was thirty-one when each married as virgins. The celebrity hype surrounding the subject, paired with Hollywood attention as in the movie comedy *The 40-Year-Old Virgin*, may be giving pause to those most influenced by popular culture—a teen audience.

A third trend has moved into focus the question of when it is appropriate to engage in sexual intercourse. More Americans than ever in the nation's history are single — 86 million, according to the most recent census data. While in 1970, 36 percent of Americans were unmarried, today's figure is 44 percent.[4] Statisticians predict that those living today to be age seventy will have spent more of their adult life single than married. Such trends do not go unnoticed even in mainline churches, where often nearly half of the members are single. In addition to wondering about and experimenting with commercial services to find a mate, Christians may begin reaching for ways and spiritual practices that help integrate their faith into the state of singlehood. What do I do in between marriages and mates? What do the scriptures or church tradition advise regarding long periods of sexual abstinence and relationship dearth? Being single is no longer the status of a few but a culturally common experience, so that it may facilitate a spiritual move from singleness toward singlemindedness in Christ.

The confluence of "celibacy chic" and the celibate liberation movement with its promises of enhanced freedom of creativity and self-actualization converge with the growing number of single Christians. Not the church but culture and socio-demographics commend the single, celibate life to Christians not merely as an option to marriage, but as an equally and perhaps even more fulfilling way of life. Paired with a sense of material oversaturation and the disappointments of sexual consumption, Christians are refocusing on matters of spirit, while rediscovering monastic practices and the spiritual disciplines of solitude, meditation, and contemplation. The quest for spiritual depth, authentic living, and a God-connectedness is gradually taking Christians to toy with, sample, and perhaps even embrace the solitary and celibate life.

In the church, the most visible, living role models for the celibate life are those who have professed its vows. Monastics, both male and female, members of religious orders, and priests are those who model for Christians the benefits and hardships of sexual abstinence. Considering that today nearly half of the members of any church or parish are single, hence called to live sexually chaste lives, it is surprising how little attention single Christians pay to those who have been practicing the vowed celibate life. The underlying assumption may be that monastics or celibate clergy are separated by a vast gulf from the common people. They have received a special grace and calling from God that eludes the rest of us. And they have been set aside as a peace offering and incarnational sacrifice before God so the rest of us common folk can do as we please.

In talking to vowed celibates I sometimes notice a reticence to acknowledge their visible, celibate witness of Christian discipleship. Is it humility or embarrassment that keeps them from discussing this vow? They may say that they couldn't do what they are doing if they were married. But there is little mention of the focused productivity and the flow of creative energies the vow has made possible for them. In looking at classic theological texts and writings on Christian spiritual practices, it soon becomes clear that many of the authors were single and celibate, or had taken religious vows.

Seeing and experiencing a celibate community in action is another venue of spiritual growth. It means witnessing how the vows translate into self-knowledge, humility, and social action on behalf of the poor and marginalized, on behalf of the sanctity of humans and creation. Each month I drive for an hour to meet my spiritual director on the campus of her religious community. I look forward to our conversations as much as I do to the chance of meeting other sisters living on the monastic grounds. In the chapel, the bookstore, and the motherhouse I observe an unreserved dedication and a handing-themselves-over to the work they do, the piety they practice, the generous compassion they exude. I understand that their "yes" to the celibate life with Christ as spouse has meant a "no" to many other things and potential loves. But their "no" has produced also a "yes," namely, the ongoing formation of Christ in them resulting from sacrifice and self-surrender, from solitude sought and saved.

The role of a celibate community is that of consolation, inspiration, and constraint. Protestant mainline churches may have singles groups, but rarely will we find a group of committed celibates, whose members meet for the purpose of accountability, encouragement, and role modeling. Over the years, I have had to piece together a circle of single women and men with whom I can talk openly about the afflictions of the body—sexual temptation and desire, romantic allure and misguided affection. I have relied on them, in lieu of a monastic community, to serve as mentors and safeguards to help me verbalize questions and bear doubts.

In Book V of the *Sayings of the Fathers* of the sixth century, an elder is sought out by a disciple who is ridden by sexual cravings. Instead of reproving and condemning him, the elder rewards his honesty with words of comfort, so that the disciple is able to return to his cell. But the troubling thoughts return, and the disciple visits the old man anew. This happens many times, with the elder repeatedly providing the following counsel: "Do not yield to the devil, nor relax your mind; rather, as often as the devil troubles you, come to me, and he shall be driven away. For nothing does discourage the demon of lust more as when his assaults are revealed. And nothing so delights him as when his imaginations are kept a secret."[5] The principle of individual confession in private or in a small group is powerful. Keeping our thoughts a secret allows temptation to fester, while exposing them to a trustworthy mentor, or a circle of them, can gradually put them to rest.

PUBLIC AND PRIVATE
COMMITMENT CEREMONIES

The step of making a public commitment to the celibate life, whether temporary or long-term, may seem like a leap. It involves an ongoing examining of one's motives and a negotiating of the line between ostentatious display and voluntary accountability. Today many Christian bookstores and mail-order catalogs feature chastity rings. The ring is touted as a tool "to help you say 'I don't' before you say 'I do'" and is sold with a pledge card to be signed and dated by the one wearing it. One of these cards reads: "I make a promise this day to God, my family, myself, my future spouse, and my future children: to remain sexually pure until the day I give myself as a wedding gift to my spouse. I know that God requires this of me, that He loves me, and that He will reward me for my faithfulness, in this life, and in the next."[6] Does wearing a chastity ring make us feel unique and superior, or is it, as the waters of baptism, an outward sign of an inward resolve and seal?

Some Christians I know have dedicated themselves in a commitment ceremony conducted by a minister or priest to live the celibate life for a period of time, or until marriage. Others have made a lifetime commitment. These women and men have taken vows in a public ceremony conducted by a bishop, have a spiritual director, and say the Liturgy of the Hours, which priests and monastics are expected to say daily; but unlike their monastic counterparts, they are not members of a religious order, they support themselves, and they may own property and live alone in their own home. An example is accountant Judith Stegman, who is one of more than fifteen thousand women worldwide recognized by the Roman Catholic Church as "consecrated virgins living in the world." Stegman was consecrated in a

1993 ceremony at St. Thomas Aquinas Church in Lansing, Michigan. But it took years of prayer meetings with other consecrated virgins and experiencing the respect others showed her before she was comfortable discussing her calling. Stegman sits on the finance committee of the Diocese of Lansing and her parish, sings in the church choir, and is on the board of several organizations, including the U.S. Association of Consecrated Virgins, of which she is president.[7]

Another practice involving celibacy and solitude is the rite of consecrated hermit. Apart from those living in monasteries, a tiny but growing number of Catholics are embracing the hermit life as it was conceived in the desert sixteen centuries ago. Not affiliated with a particular religious order, members are Christian men and women, some with children, marriages, and lucrative careers in their past. They choose solitude, celibacy, and asceticism in order to focus full time on God.

WEDDED CHASTITY

The spiritual practice of the celibate life is not reserved for single people. The Apostle Paul commended to couples in the Corinthian church temporary abstinence from sexual relations, provided both partners were in agreement. "Do not deprive one another except perhaps by agreement for a set time," he writes, "to devote yourselves to prayer, and then come together again, so that Satan may not tempt you because of your lack of self-control" (1 Cor. 7:5). With the high regard for celibacy during the first five centuries of Christianity, marital celibacy evolved as a similar ideal. In a sermon on the parable of the ten virgins in Matthew 25:1–13, St. Augustine says that all Christians are virgins—not just women and men of holy orders or clergy—and are to act accordingly. All are to use their five senses properly by abstaining from "unlawful seeing, unlawful hearing, unlawful smelling, unlawful tasting, and unlawful touching" and carry the lamps of their good works. Foolish virgins are those who practice abstinence and good works to please others, while the wise virgins carry "the inner oil of conscience" and on the last day will find themselves in the "spiritual embrace" of the Bridegroom.[8]

As Christians we view our bodies as receptacles of Christ's image, conduits of the Spirit, creations of God's design. Practicing solitude means to guard against outside forces, influences, and dependencies for the sake of keeping the body pure and available to God in Christ. The examples of men and women of past and present practicing solitude, even from nonreligious motives, help us become attentive to what goes in our bodies, whose company we keep, and with what (and with whom) we unite. They guide us in discerning who and what "is not good for us." And they model for us a countercultural type of courage that guards and regards the human body as the locus of the Word become flesh.

19

Charting the Landscape of the Soul

The purpose of spiritual disciplines is to set up the outer conditions for an inner exploration. Detachment from the material world by "confining" the ego or by personal or communal "rules" (commitment to and observance of particular practices) is not aimed at repressing and sublimating important desires and feelings, but at expanding our awareness of another landscape, the landscape of our soul. Refraining from instant gratification, postponing physical closeness and union when we long for the company of another, distancing ourselves from the promises of intimacy ultimately benefit our soul. Not fear of the physical world, but its transcendence and a desire for the spiritual world are at stake. Not avoidance of contact with others, but union with God is what is sought.

By putting ourselves in a position we would not commonly prefer, under conditions that may not be to our temporary liking, we are able to develop a desire for them and experience, what Father Zosima in Dostoyevsky's *The Brothers Karamazov* called "the yoke of liberty." Our willingness to take on this "yoke" is preceded by a faith in the long-term benefits that emerge with repeated practice. Whether it is learning to play a musical instrument, speak a foreign language, or paint with oils, we submit ourselves to practice in hopes of gaining eventual mastery and experiencing the joys of new vistas and creativity. Practicing God's presence by making room for God in solitude, detachment, and surrender is an ongoing, dynamic activity. We lose the sense of God's presence when we skirt the practices or when we apply them without thought, preparation, or self-awareness. It is then that spiritual practices grow mechanical, hollow, stale. The incentive for spiritual practice is the hope of things unseen, accompanied by a sense of and admission to our weakness in the face of bodily impulses. The paradox is constant: the tension between experiencing the discomfort of the practice and acknowledging the importance of things other than the immediate, temporary gratification of our senses and needs.

What then is the spiritual life and what are the practices directed primarily at the soul? According to theologian John Macquarrie, the realm of the spirit in humans is "that extra dimension of being" that makes us more than mere physical organisms and that provides us with openness, freedom, self-transcendence, and creativity. The spirit's direction is a moving away from the ego toward a "going out and spending [of] itself," so that the more the spiritual life is deepened, the more we become truly human — and the more we grow in likeness to God, who is Spirit.[1] Spiritual practices help us heighten the awareness of this invisible "extra dimension of being." They bring into focus the false ego that has absorbed the place of God in us so we can steer clear of it, die to it, and make room for the Spirit of God to move in and do its transformative work. The practices of meditative prayer, mystical seeing, and apophatic and kataphatic worship, among others, move us into taking a solitary position before God where being alone can produce a sense of "becoming all one" — with people, nature, and God.

MEDITATIVE PRAYER

If seeing is believing, then believing is seeing with new eyes. During Jesus' ministry, many people followed him because they had witnessed his miracles and healings: they could see and therefore they believed. But Jesus was teaching his disciples the reverse: believing is seeing. Through the lens of faith a new kingdom reality emerges where the vistas are splendid and extravagant and vast because a divine hand has drawn them. Through earthly, faith-filled eyes we glimpse heavenly reality, thus weaving together heaven and earth. Keeping our faith lens polished means to continually feed on what renews and invigorates our faith.

Meditative prayer helps us do so by readjusting and re-orienting our entire self — mind, body, and spirit — to God for proper seeing.

One of the most influential and prolific twentieth-century writers on the spiritual life and meditative prayer is the Trappist monk and hermit Thomas Merton, O.C.S.O. (1915–68). After a dissolute life of social and sexual activity, Merton experienced a conversion and entered the monastery at the Abbey of Our Lady of Gethsemani, near Louisville, Kentucky, in 1941. The order was formally called the Order of the Cistercians of the Strict Observance, a strict Roman Catholic order devoted to communal prayer (spending at least four hours a day in chapel, chanting the Psalms), to private prayer and contemplation, to study, and to manual labor. Except for those whose special duties required otherwise, they vowed not to speak except in singing the praises of God.

The Trappist life followed the Rule of St. Benedict, which said that being a hermit was the highest form of spiritual endeavor. But for nearly a thousand years the hermit tradition was virtually unpracticed in the church, and Merton, who was involved in monastic renewal, wanted to change that. He himself sought the life of the modern hermit, and for years argued with his abbot on this question. When Merton was in his seventeenth year at the Abbey of Gethsemani the abbot finally allowed a hermitage to be built in the forest near the monastery. It was a primitive unheated dwelling, without toilet or kitchen. Merton was allowed to go there for a few hours a day, and then gradually a little more, and finally in late 1965, three years before his accidental death in Bangkok, Thailand, to live there full time. Merton rejoiced in the hermit's life. Each day he would get up at about 2:30 a.m., go through a lengthy Trappist routine of prayers and meditation, and then begin a rigorous day of writing.[2]

Merton's quest for solitude, contemplation, and the spiritual life is fully developed in his writing. In *Thoughts in Solitude,* written in 1953–54 and published in 1956, Merton links the spiritual life with solitude in sustained meditative prayer. "To keep ourselves spiritually alive we must constantly renew our faith." For "we are like pilots of fog-bound steamers, peering into the gloom in front of us, listening for the sounds of other ships, and we can only reach the harbor if we keep alert." The "spiritual life is, then, first of all a matter of keeping awake." Meditative prayer is one of the ways in which the spiritual person stays awake. But it should not be surprising that those aspiring to religious perfection "grow dull and fall asleep," for "meditative prayer is a stern discipline, and one which cannot be learned by violence. It requires unending courage and perseverance, and those who are not willing to work at it patiently will finally end in compromise," which is "another name for failure."[3]

For Merton, to meditate is to think. Yet meditation is much more than reasoning and thinking, more than affections and a series of prepared acts. In prayer, one thinks and speaks not only with one's mind and lips, but with one's whole being. "It is the orientation of our whole body, mind, and spirit to God in silence, attention, and adoration. All good meditative prayer is conversion of our entire self to God."[4]

Meditative prayer is difficult because it prompts "a kind of inner upheaval," according to Merton. Generally people avoid this type of upheaval and are incapable of the effort required to make it. They are ineffective in prayer because they lack generosity toward God or direction and experience. At the same time, they "disturb themselves [and] throw themselves into agitation by the violent efforts they make" and "they end in hopelessness." Such efforts at prayer are a compromise, resulting in "a series of frustrated routines which help them to pass the time, or else they relax into a state of semi-coma which, they hope, can be justified by the name of contemplation."[5] In addition, there is also the peril that we depend too much on our imagination and emotions in prayer. We "plunge into a riot of images and fabricate for ourselves our own home-made religious experience." What we need to do, instead, is go looking for God's presence in the very center of our humility, in the very depths of our spiritual nature. It is here that we can sense "a certain presence of self to Self" in which we know "Him in Whom all things have their being." And it is here that we can sense "a very real and very recognizable (but almost entirely indefinable) Presence of God, in which we confront Him in prayer knowing Him by Whom we are known, aware of Him Who is aware of us, loving Him by Whom we know ourselves to be loved."[6]

The period of 1951 to 1959 is commonly viewed as Merton's attempt to work renewal in the Christian monastic tradition by promoting the eremitic life. Toward the end of this period, Merton makes the shift from promoting solitude for monastics to solitude for all Christians. "Not all men are called to be hermits, but all men need enough silence and solitude in their lives to enable the deep inner voice of their own true self to be heard at least occasionally," he says. For one cannot go on happily for long, unless one is in contact with the springs of spiritual life which are hidden in the depths of one's own true soul.[7]

For Merton solitude is not a condition, but an activity. It is "a realization, an actualization, even a kind of creation, as well as a liberation of active forces within us, forces that are more than our own, and yet more ours than what appears to be 'ours.'" When solitude is a mere condition, it is passive and unreal, and it resembles a "kind of permanent coma" with a "phony purpose." Hence one has to work at it to keep out of this condition by "some kind of technique of integration that keeps body and soul together, harmonizes their powers, brings them out into one deep resonance." There is a need for presence, concentration, emptiness—all aspects of a "realized solitude." It is only through such ongoing, concentrated efforts of integration that the false self built up by the pressures and stratagems of society is unmasked.

At the same time, the true self is uncovered also. Living into such realized solitude takes us into the wilderness of the human spirit and of God. "The real wilderness of the hermit," says Merton, "is the wilderness of the human spirit which is at once his and everyone else's. What he seeks in that wilderness is not himself, not human company and consolation, but God." Our loneliness, whether sought in prayer or meditation or contemplation, reconstructs the loneliness of God. "This is why it is such a great thing for a man to discover his solitude and learn to live in it. For there he finds that he and God are one: that God is aloneness as he himself is alone. That God wills to be alone in man."[8] Meditative prayer prepares and prompts us to consciously enter into the process of upheaval and conversion of our entire self toward God. Thereby, we are confronted with our aloneness and taught to live there. By cultivating our solitude in the wilderness of the soul, our aloneness converges with the aloneness of God, drawing spirit to Spirit and uniting the two as one.

MYSTICAL VISION, MYSTICAL UNION

At a weeklong retreat on Christian mystics, the presenter introduced us during the first session to the spiritual landscape of the soul. Mystics, she said, are people who may be living in and are fully engaged with the world, but they bring to it a larger perspective. They have seen and been to a place that defies description and is rarely glimpsed by those of us absorbed in and driven by the day-to-day affairs of business, work, and appearances. With that she held up an enlarged black-and-white photograph of an iceberg. The small tip was exposed above the waters, but its huge and solid body—at least seven times the size of the iceberg's tip— was underwater. The spiritual life is concerned with dipping beneath the surface and exploring the vast underwater topography of the iceberg. Most often we dive under only when our exploration of the visible tip has come to a forced standstill, when there is no exit, and we have nowhere left to go but down and inward, into an invisible world.

In the introduction to her book *Christian Mystics*, Ursula King defines a mystic as a person who is deeply aware of the presence of the divine Spirit. "Mystics often perceive the presence of God throughout the world of nature and all that is alive," she says, "leading to a transfiguration of the ordinary all around them." Their story is one of a "passionate love affair between human beings and God," and it "speaks of deep yearning, of burning desire for the contemplation and presence of the divine beloved." Their quest is for union with God; their mystical experience is one of "spiritual consciousness," where all "other relationships count as nothing when compared with the relationship of the soul to God."[9] In her study of sixty mystics, King includes the Trappist monk and hermit Charles de Foucauld, the British Jesuit Gerard Manley Hopkins, the mystical poet and scholar Evelyn Underhill, the German Carmelite nun and philosopher Edith Stein, the Swedish economist and statesman Dag Hammarskjöld, along with the French Jewish writer Simone Weil and the French Jesuit paleontologist Pierre Teilhard de Chardin. "The best-known modern mystic," according to King, though, is Thomas Merton, who is "one of the most influential contemporary spiritual writers."[10]

Merton was deeply familiar with mystical thought in the Christian tradition. He had published *The Wisdom of the Desert* in 1960, a collection of the sayings of the desert fathers; had written his graduate thesis at Columbia on "Nature and Art in William Blake"; had drawn on the writings of John of the Cross and Julian of Norwich in *New Seeds of Contemplation* (1962) and in *Contemplative Prayer* (published posthumously in 1969); and had been living by the Rule of St. Benedict. The interior journey begins, says Merton in a 1966 letter, when "people realize that life can have an interior dimension of depth and awareness which is systematically blocked by our habitual way of life, all concentrated on externals." It begins with acknowledging "the poverty of a life fragmented and dispersed in things and built on a superficial idea of the self and its relation to what is outside and around it." There is a "need to open up an inner freedom and vision, which is found in relatedness to something in us which we don't really know." The inner life and freedom of the person "begin when this inner dimension opens up and man lives in communion with the unknown in him."[11]

In *Contemplation in a World of Action,* posthumously published in 1971, Merton had advised on how to find the real world. It is not merely by measuring and observing what is outside us, but by discovering our own inner ground. "For that is where the world is, first of all: in my deepest self. This 'ground,' this 'world' where I am mysteriously present at once to my own self and to the freedoms of all other men, is not a visible and determined structure with fixed laws and demands. It is a living and self-creating mystery of which I am myself a part, to which I am myself my own

unique door."[12] And in a 1967 letter to Dom Francis Decroix, written at the request of Pope Paul VI for a "message
of contemplatives to the world," Merton explains the fun-
damental message of the contemplative and mystic. It is
"to reassure you and say that if you dare to penetrate your
own silence and risk the sharing of that solitude with the
lonely other who seeks God through you, then you will truly
recover the light and the capacity to understand what is
beyond words," namely, "the intimate union in the depths
of your own heart, of God's spirit and your own secret in-
most self, so that you and He are in all truth One Spirit."[13]
In a letter written the following day to Dom Francis, Merton adds that the mystical way is not reserved to a few.
All people "can seek and find this intimate awareness and
awakening which is a gift of love and a vivifying touch of
creative and redemptive power, that power which raised
Christ from the dead and cleanses us from dead works to
serve the living God."[14]

By the end of our retreat on mysticism, we had spent the
majority of time immersed in the thoughts and writings of
such mystics as Meister Eckhart, Julian of Norwich, Thomas
Merton, Karl Rahner, and Etty Hillesum. We had also immersed ourselves, except for a few hours during and after
dinner, in silence — while eating, studying, journaling, or
passing one another during walks along the beach. Words
were temporarily replaced by gentle nods, smiles, gestures,
and an occasional whisper. Then the silence began to grow
loud, resounding with the echoes of what had caught my attention during the morning lecture, at morning prayers or
evening vespers or daily Mass, in my room or on the beach
along the lake or on the grounds while gazing and reading
and taking notes. The communal silence produced in me
a solitary song, a resonance that arose slowly, gently, and

unmistakably, speaking without words the sound of comfort, an assurance of presence, a sense of privilege to be allowed to participate in something beautiful and dynamically whole. The lecture on the retreat's last day was on the mystic in each of us. During each of the preceding sessions, a picture of the mystic we were studying was on display. That day there was a framed mirror. The presenter picked it up and while slowly walking our circle held it up to us at eye level, so we could see our reflection. "You are a mystic," she said. "Take a good look at this face. God is inviting you to deeper union with him." It was an invitation to enter the life of the spirit.

PRAYING WITH EYES CLOSED AND WIDE OPEN

There are two mystical traditions in the life of prayer. One tradition is concerned with the emptying of one's mind of all ideas, images, sensations; it is often called "apophatic" prayer, implying a movement upward and "away from" (the meaning of the Greek word *apo*) the earthly, the material, the concrete. The other tradition is given to the prayerful use of concrete images, such as icons, symbols, ritual, sacrament, and the engaging of the imagination; it is called kataphatic prayer, because it employs what is "down" here (from the Greek word *kata,* down) and what can be perceived by our senses. According to Thomas Keating, O.C.S.O., it is misleading to juxtapose the two forms of prayer. To him, kataphatic prayer is simply a preparation for contemplation, the opening of mind and heart to God "beyond thoughts, words, and emotions." Apophatic prayer, on the other hand, is "true contemplation" because it is a resting in God beyond the exercise of particular acts or visualization exercises, "beyond our ordinary human faculties of thinking and feeling."[15]

Perhaps the most traditional way of cultivating apophatic prayer is Lectio Divina. In this prayer practice one listens to a Bible text as if one were in conversation with God and God were suggesting the topics and themes of discussion. The act of listening to God occurs in three stages: pondering the words, engaging them emotionally, and allowing these thoughts, responses, and feelings to calm down and to eventually produce a quiet resting in God. This process can be compared to moving from communicating to communing with God, where, much like in human relationships between intimate friends, one can sit in silence and enjoy the other's company without saying a word.

Eugene Peterson takes a different approach. "Kataphatic prayer is 'praying with our eyes open,' " he says, while "apophatic prayer is 'praying with our eyes closed.' At our balanced best, the two traditions intermingle, mix, and cross-fertilize."[16] This means we are comfortable hearing the words of scripture proclaimed, engaging with them, and allowing them to take us to a quiet place of "blessed assurance," where we know to be in God's loving company. And it means we are equally comfortable at allowing visuals, rituals, drama, and objects of art to take us by the hand to lead us into an encounter with the divine. Most of us are not usually at our balanced best. In my own tradition, the Protestant church, we tend to lean heavily toward the apophatic. We close our eyes and shut out the natural world, along with eliminating or delimiting objects of art or ritual or dance as prayer tools to keep our senses pure, undefiled, and disengaged. The reticence among Protestants to use the visual or performing arts (other than music) to support worship is a result of the apophatic emphasis.

Instead of enhancements, they are regarded as worldly distractions that, if not carefully employed, might lure the faithful down the pernicious path of idol worship.

My own experience differs in that regard. I grew up attending Mass every Sunday, sitting with other girls and women on the left side of the church's center aisle, the "Mary section" as we called it, and watching the mysterious dance of acolytes and priest. I can still feel the drops of holy water land on my hair and cheek during the sprinkling rite at the opening of Mass, smell the incense and the flowers that decorated the chancel, hear the sanctus bells, see the Mary statue's serene eyes and the thick layer of purple hydrangeas hiding her bare feet. The wooden crucifix with its life-size corpus, the towering gilded altar piece, the ceiling paintings teeming with naked angels in this old, German country church built in Gothic style drew me up and into another place, another time.

No one told me what these art works were to help me do; they just did it: they alerted me to another, other-worldly realm and set a tiny prayer wheel in motion in my child-sized heart. I not only believed but *knew* that God lived in this splendid place filled with gold and flowers, flickering candles and echoing organ, Latin liturgy and the Blessed Host. I don't ever remember our family being late for church. By the time the bells were ringing for the third time — the longest and loudest of the three cycles urging latecomers to hustle — I was in the children's pew up front directly beneath the bells' din, gazing at Mary and sniffing the strange smells of God's presence. To me, church was a place like no other — a mix between the secret hideout in the thick, dark pine forest behind our house and the interior of a King Ludwig castle with its expansive mirror room that glistened with semiprecious stones and sparkling crystal. Church back then was a veritable feast of smell, color, motion, and sound that stroked me, woke me, and spoke to me of the secret, mysterious wonder and the awesome, express splendor of God. It also spoke to me of a God who was both concealed and revealed, silent and vocal, elusive and in plain view.

Today, working in a Presbyterian congregation I am grateful for its balance of both traditions. While steeped in the apophatic prayer practice, its worship contains many kataphatic elements—the drama of liturgy patterned after the *Book of Common Worship,* the colorful stained-glass windows lining our sanctuary with depictions of biblical characters and Gospel scenes, the carved images of the four evangelists at the tips of our wooden chancel cross. I am also grateful for our church's liturgical dance group, one I am privileged to be part of, that seeks to enhance worship by dancing to hymns and visually interpreting through rhythmic movement and gesture a poem or a biblical text.

The use of religious images and icons in both public and private worship can be a powerful prayer tool. Incidentally, many of the traditional Christian symbols invite us to reflect on our solitary state before God and to come, as the old-time Gospel hymn has it, "to the garden alone." For example, the focal point of most sanctuaries and churches is the cross, whose beams intersect in one solitary point, a symbol of the unique intersection within our body of the divine with the human, of the eternal with the temporal, of heaven with earth, of life with death. There is also the crucifix, on which Christ hangs abandoned and alone to die, unaided by his family and community, deserted by both friend and foe. And there is the picture of the Virgin Mary with child, symbol of the celibate God-bearer, who had conceived a child in isolation and apart from intimacy and sexual union with a man, and who had to bear alone the death threats, derision, and suspicion over her pregnancy.

Like icons, these symbols participate in the historical reality of what they depict as well as taking us beyond that reality to the transcendent and divine reality in Christ.

BEING ALONE AS BECOMING "ALL ONE"

Contemplating our aloneness is a frightening experience. The desert fathers and mystics called the monastic cell their paradise and place of peace as well as their purgatory. Aloneness means we have nothing else to face but ourselves, our shortcomings, our unforgiving attitude. According to David Steindl-Rast, O.S.B., the cell is "the inescapable symbol of the truth that we are, in a real way, 'alone with the Alone.'" It uncovers what is true for all of us, namely, that "deep in our heart we are alone with the Alone." But this is not the end. For "mysteriously, the word 'alone' can be read as 'all one.' When we face our aloneness, when we enter our heart of hearts and confront God, we are united with all."[17] While our aloneness confronts us with death and the need to let go of the place reserved for God, it also takes us beyond death unto a new life, the resurrection with Christ that unites us with all things and with God.

The mystical life, leading to union with all things and with God, is often called the contemplative life. But such contemplation has little to do with concentrated and protracted periods of meditation. According to Steindl-Rast, the word "contemplation" "literally means a continuous putting together according to some measure." In contemplation, he says, we connect the two realms of the temporal and the eternal, of *chronos* and *kairos,* of time on earth and time in heaven. In other words, we "measure what we are doing in time against the now that doesn't pass away." Traditional Christian spirituality calls this merging of both spheres *sub specie aeternitatis,* a retrieving amid the temporal "the point of view of eternity."[18] Since our lives have depth and meaning only when viewed from a higher vantage point, contemplation invites us to consider our temporal concerns and suffering in light of the eternal now. "For those who want to save their life will lose it," Jesus said, but "those who lose their life for my sake will save it" (Luke 9:24). By loosening our firm grip on life, by contemplatively measuring our present pain and discomfort against the eternal now, we are "losing our life" and entering into solitude before God in whom the temporal and the eternal converge and connect and unite.

In a scientific age, perhaps the most significant Christian mystic is the one taking us back full circle to the vision of ultimate union of spirit and matter, of heaven and earth, in Christ. How does one arrive at such a unifying vision, and what are the practices involved? One of the mystics to chart the course for us is the eminent researcher, biologist, and paleontologist Pierre Teilhard de Chardin, S.J. (1881–1955). Widely known and respected for his scientific work, this Jesuit priest was forbidden to teach or publish his theological thoughts during his lifetime. The Roman Catholic Church considered them unorthodox and dangerous. When within the year of his death *The Phenomenon of Man* was published, it became an immediate bestseller. Between 1955 and 1976 all of Teilhard's books and essays appeared in thirteen volumes in the original French version. Most of them have been translated into English, but much of Teilhard's writings remains misunderstood or underappreciated.

According to Ursula King, Teilhard is "one of the least well known and most ignored spiritual writers of the present age" and "one of the least understood and most misquoted thinkers of the twentieth century."[19] Combining the scientific and the spiritual, Teilhard's vision may be unprecedented in Christian thought for opening up the union of spirit and matter, of the soul and flesh. In the rhythm of life and its dynamic evolutionary progress, at the center of the cosmos and the world, Teilhard saw a divine center, a living heart beating with the fiery energy of love and compassion. This living heart was God in Christ, brought together in the three dimensions of the cosmic, the human, and the Christic. These three dimensions consisted of the heart of matter, of the world, and of God and they were all one and the same. At their core, they were Christ's heart, the image of God's outpouring of life and love that pulsated throughout the entirety of creation.

For those of us marked by Western tradition's dualism of spirit and matter, it is difficult to embrace the sacredness of matter in creation. I enjoy gardening, for example, and the activities of digging and weeding, planting and staking, dividing clumps of root and trimming stalks. Years ago I read that talking to plants enhances their health, and so I talk to my plants, lately including in my "conversations" even the rocks in my flowerbed and the soil. Still, while I talk to flowers, rocks, and soil out of respect for their being, I do so not without first glancing over my shoulder to be sure I am alone. Native American traditions make no apologies for acknowledging the sacredness of matter. A prayer of the Objibway people is: "Grandfather, Sacred One, teach us love, compassion, and honor, that we may heal the earth and heal each other."[20] Chief Seattle says, "If men spit upon the earth they spit upon themselves."[21] And the Sioux people pray, "May I never deceive mother earth, may I never deceive other people, may I never deceive myself, and above all may I never deceive you."[22]

Teilhard's work as a paleontologist made him deeply reverent of matter, both for its possibilities and threatening force. In the essay "Hymn to Matter," he praises matter for its qualities of revealing the Christ of the universe. "Blessed be you, mighty matter, irresistible march of evolution, reality ever newborn; you who, by constantly shattering our mental categories, force us to go ever further and further in our pursuit of the truth.... Blessed be you, impenetrable matter: you who, interposed between our minds and the world of essences, cause us to languish with the desire to pierce through the seamless veil of phenomena.... Raise me up then, matter, to those heights, through struggle and separation and death; raise me up until, at long last, it becomes possible for me in perfect chastity to embrace the universe."[23]

For Teilhard, the elements of such "chastity" consist of an unremitting surrender to the boundaries, obstacles, and visible limitations in the act of solitude and detachment. By its limiting and unyielding force, matter — which includes the human body — trains us to submit to God in worship. In the "Cosmic Life," he describes this vision. "Every encounter that brings me a caress, that spurs me on, that comes as a shock to me, that bruises or breaks me," he says, "is a contact with the hand of God, which assumes countless forms and yet always commands our worship." Even our human body and every "element of which I am made up is an overflow from God," so that when "I surrender myself to the embrace of the visible and tangible universe, I am able to be in communion with the invisible that purifies, and to incorporate myself in the Spirit without blemish."[24]

Practicing solitude and detachment leads to an increased vision of union with all things. In the paradox of separating ourselves from the external world, we find ourselves and the true ground of our being, God. "The deeper I descend into myself," says Teilhard, "the more I find God at the heart of my being; the more I multiply the links that attach me to

things, the more closely does he hold me." It is "when I obe-
diently lose myself in your vast folds, [that] I am immersed
in God's creative action, whose hand has never ceased...to
mold the human clay that is destined to constitute the Body
of his Son." Such detachment also produces an increased
acceptance of self, our blemishes and faults, and even the
blows and unexpected turns of events that come our way.
Teilhard writes: I can "bless the vicissitudes, the good for-
tune, the misadventures of my career." I can "bless my own
character, my virtues, my faults...my blemishes." And I can
"love my own self, in the form in which it was given to me
and in the form in which my destiny molds me. What is
more, I strive to guess and anticipate the lightest breezes
that call to me, so that I may spread my sails more widely
to them."[25]

According to Teilhard, spirit and matter are not fused
but intricately interrelated. They are two directions within
the evolution of the world, whose beginning and end is
Christ, the Alpha and the Omega. This creative, dynamic
union can be seen only from the spiritual perspective, from
a position of prayerful adoration. By its nature, "science
is necessarily chiefly concerned with studying the material arrangements" and thus "it sees only the outer crust of
things." The "true evolution of the world," however, "takes
place in souls and in their union. Its inner factors are not
mechanistic but psychological and moral," so that true con-
sistence and the reality of what is does not come from
matter, but from spirit.[26]

To attain this view of two converging entities in Christ,
the cosmic union of matter and spirit, takes a proper spiritual practice. This practice urges us to see the world and
ourselves in it as a divine milieu. In his essay *Le Milieu
Divin,* Teilhard teaches his readers the practical attitude of

how to see. "Leave the surface" of things "without leaving the world" and wholeheartedly "plunge into God."[27] "Place yourself here," he says, "and look from this privileged position — which is no hard-won height reserved for the elect, but the solid platform built by two thousand years of Christian experience." Then you will see "without mixture, without confusion, the true God, the Christian God, [who] will under your gaze invade the universe, our universe of today, the universe which so frightened you by its alarming size or its pagan beauty. He will penetrate it as a ray of light does a crystal and, with the help of the great layers of creation, he will become for you universally perceptible and active — very near and very distant at one and the same time."[28]

Central to receiving this unifying Christic vision is that we discern the false self, the ego. It is a process quickened by prayer and participation in the Eucharist. Teilhard gives ample evidence of this process by the numerous prayers scattered throughout his theological writings and the importance to him of the consecrated body and blood of Christ. When living in the trenches during World War I without the opportunity to participate in or to say Mass, Teilhard wrote a "Mass on Things," which he later renamed "The Mass on the World." "Lord Jesus," says Teilhard, "now that beneath those world-forces you have become truly and physically everything for me . . . , I shall gather into a single prayer both my delight in what I have and my thirst for what I lack."[29] Through this particular offering of the Mass he not only sought to express his vision of a unified cosmos whose center and end were Christ, but he also offered up himself as a living sacrifice. "For me, my God, all joy and all achievements, the very purpose of my being and all my love of life, all depend on this one basic vision of the union between yourself and the universe. Let others, fulfilling a function more august than mine, proclaim your splendors as pure spirit; as for me...I have no desire, I have no ability, to proclaim anything except the innumerable prolongations of your incarnate being in the world of matter."[30] To that end, then, "Lord, lock me up in the deepest depths of your heart; and then, holding me there, burn me, purify me, set me on fire, sublimate me, till I become utterly what you would have me be, through the utter annihilation of my ego."[31]

By transcending the "matter" of the ego, the illusionary self, Teilhard could see Christ in all things in heaven and on earth, in both matter and spirit, not divided and polarized in competition with each other, but as two directions moving and evolving toward one center, one point. Teilhard called this point the Omega Christ, in whom we — and all of creation and the entire universe — live and move and have our being and find fulfillment and joy and rest. It is a vision not reserved for the few or elect but one granted to those who submit their consciences to the scrutiny of God, those ever vigilant to discern and relinquish the illusionary self and to die to self, those yielding in aloneness to the Alone — the Christ — in whom all things evolve and rise and converge as one.

Conclusion

The classical practices of solitude were formed and established largely within the first five centuries of Christianity. By trial and error, early Christians sought distinct ways that would allow for Christ to be formed in them. Acts of mercy, almsgiving, service to the community through the exercise of one's spiritual and material gifts were aimed at building up the body of Christ, the church. At the center of the quest was the responsibility of each believer to present one's heart and conscience to God for ongoing scrutiny. The Christian way of life became the way in which Christ was formed in the heart. Taking responsibility for the heart and the inner landscape of the soul was up to the individual. The community served as mirror, enforcer, forecaster, or accountability agent of sorts. The will of the individual was at stake, the internal place and crucible where Christ could take shape as the new creation. The cell was the place of confinement, the locus of investigation and formation. Vows were the outer signs of a reality inwardly perceived and realized. The earliest vows in Western Christianity evolved gradually and gained formal acceptance in Benedictine monastic practice. Poverty, celibacy, obedience, and stability served as tools for keeping the disciple on course. The aim was individual spiritual formation. The practitioners were those who had responded to the call to the monastic communal life.

Today Christians are seeking a more intimate walk with God. The promises of affluence and consumption, the freedom of career adventure and sexual exploration have not met the spiritual thirst. The simplicity and singlehearted focus of the monastic way of life is gaining popularity among a wider audience. Monastic practices of meditation, contemplation, and short-term or long-term vows have spread beyond the monastery walls. A new kind of disciple has emerged, one who is living in the world and following a rule that is a composite of monastic or desert tradition and individual quest. For lack of immediate communal guidelines, it may be harder for this type of disciple to succeed at Christian formation. It takes active networking, mentors,

spiritual guides, and perhaps a group of like-minded seekers to serve as mirror and accountability agents. But this
communal lack may also produce a more reflected quest
and authentic recovery, beyond routine and vain ritual, of
the questions each of us brings to God.

Now as then, the Jesus of history in the Gospels and the
Christ of faith in the histories and autobiographies of his
followers call us to present our offerings and questions to
him. It is this Jesus, the Christ, who gives us glimpses of the
landscape of the soul. It is he who invites us to the practices of contemplation and meditative prayer. He calls us to
imitate him by following him into death, a repeated death
to our affections, emotional ties, and need to control. He invites us to contemplate the mystery of death that prepares a
way to new life in him. And he invites us to meditate on our
pain and to sit with it long enough to allow it to transform
and mold us into something as yet unknown and unseen.

Christian mystics and monastics of past and present can
tell us what to expect. They have gone before us, providing
assurance that the path is not in vain, holds promise, yields
gain, namely—a glimpse of the union of all things on earth
and in heaven, uniting pain and joy, loss and gain, creature and creation within the heart of Christ. One of these
mystics and monastics is Richard Rohr, O.F.M. Having ad-
mired Thomas Merton for a long time, Rohr decided one
day to spend a thirty-day retreat at Merton's hermitage in
Bardstown, Kentucky, living, as Merton might have done,
without books, radio, or TV. "I thought that if I were at his
place," writes Rohr, "I might be able to incorporate some
of his wisdom. And so I managed to spend the spring in the
foothills of Kentucky, absolutely alone with myself, with the
woods, and, I hoped, with God." Rohr figured it would be
"deadly boring" and not "especially edifying." In the morning he watched the sun come up, in the evening he watched

it go down, with only a diary by his side. Then one evening, "I laid my finger on my cheek and found to my surprise that it was wet. I wondered what those tears meant. What was I crying for? I wasn't consciously sad at all or consciously happy. I noticed at this moment that behind it all there was a joy, deeper than any personal joy. It was a joy in the face of the beauty of being." At the same moment, he also experienced the exact opposite emotion. "I hadn't known before that two such contrary feelings could coexist. Because the tears were at the same time tears of an immense sadness, a sadness at what we're doing to the earth, sadness at the people whom I have already hurt in my life, and a sadness too at my own emptiness and stupidity."[1]

In solitude we discover the place where we are united with God already, the vision of the new Reign of God, the landscape that weaves heaven and earth into one. And as we expose ourselves to this state of temporary confinement and "prison living," setting aside our grumbling and need to control, we allow for the space to emerge into which God can move. All of us will need cheerleaders and tour guides in this endeavor, for it is daunting to enter, difficult to stay put, and hard to return there of our own free will. Gently and lovingly these guides beckon, and in prose and poetry they call. In a poem introducing the way of the solitary life, Thomas Merton invites us to look beyond our hesitation and to listen and yield to the kind voice of Solitude:

> Follow my ways and I will lead you
> To golden-haired suns,
> Logos and music, blameless joys,
> Innocent of questions
> And beyond answers.
> For I, Solitude, am thine own Self:

> I, Nothingness, am thy All.
> I, Silence, am thy Amen.[2]

Solitude, nothingness, and silence are ways of being: being alone, being nothing, being silent. They capture elements of existence, not activity; of being, not doing, and point to ways of becoming more human, more whole. It is a great paradox. What seems to limit our self-expression brings us to a deeper expression of self. What appears to confine prepares us for new freedom. What appears like death births life. It is also our great hope: that in our aloneness we meet the Alone, that in our humility we meet the one who humbled himself even unto death, that in our silence we meet the one who speaks without words as the Word. By surrendering to this solitary encounter, we are taken to the center of ourselves, the world, and the universe where matter and spirit, flesh and soul, I and neighbor beat as "all one" in the heart of the One who lives in us.

Acknowledgments

Writing is a solitary endeavor, painful and exhilarating, dislocating and centering, trying and calming at the same time. In the end, the lonesome journey has its rewards and we can look back in gratitude and detect the wonder of the unexpected spirit-filled guideposts that have parted the waters for us and granted us safe passage on relatively dry ground. Many people have left their imprint in the way of birthing this book, leading me through valleys and grafting safe passageways. I thank the members of the First Presbyterian Church of Ann Arbor for their open, curious, and critical minds and generous hearts in responding to sermons and lectures, and for their passion in our work together in Christ's behalf. I thank the readers of the rough draft and the listeners of my fledgling ideas for their honest feedback and their insights and inspiration by who they are in light of God's grace, David Bucholtz, Alice Camille, Ron Case, Lorraine Duarte, Paul Simpson Duke, Sarah Hart, Robert Hater, Antje Pohmer, and Laura Smit.

I thank those who throughout the process were models to me in exegetical exactitude and pastoral practicality — Astrid Beck, Ursula King, Carol Muehlig, Eugene Peterson, and Roland Rolheiser — and who guided me by their theological reasoning, profundity, and poetic depth. I thank my spiritual director, Margaret Gaffney, I.H.M., for her patience and optimism in being to me mirror and mold, and Margaret Brennan, I.H.M., for leading me into the underwater vistas of the soul's landscape at a retreat on the mystics and for mentoring me one-on-one. Much credit for this book goes to the editorial team at the Crossroad Publishing

Company, my copyeditor Shirley Coe and typesetter John Eagleson, and the person who prodded me to write, parlayed ideas, and practiced patience, Roy M. Carlisle, senior editor at Crossroad. He has been to me both compassionate critic and passionate collaborator, wise friend and vigorous force from the book's humble beginnings in the initial, now deleted, pages of the writing warmup to its closing chapter.

This book is dedicated to those who persevere against all odds, those who labor without the prospect of applause, those who have dived under and are swimming against culture's currents and tidal waves as Christ's subversive workforce in the depths of solitude, silence, and surrender.

Notes

Chapter 1 / Longing for Eyes

1. Rainer Maria Rilke, *The Book of Hours: Prayers to a Lowly God*, trans. Annemarie S. Kidder (Evanston, IL: Northwestern University Press, 2001), 159.

Chapter 2 / I Need My Space

1. Rainer Maria Rilke, letter to Emanuel von Bodman, Westerwede, August 17, 1901; trans. Stephen Mitchell in Stephen Mitchell, *The Essence of Wisdom* (New York: Broadway Books, 1999), 43.

2. See John R. Landgraf, *Singling: A New Way to Live the Single Life* (Louisville: Westminster/John Knox Press, 1990), esp. 20–21.

3. Ibid., 18.

4. Ibid., 19.

5. Rilke, letter to von Bodman, 43.

6. *The American Heritage Dictionary of the English Language* (Boston: Houghton Mifflin, 1969).

Chapter 3 / What Are These Words That You Are Exchanging?

1. Eugene H. Peterson, *Under the Unpredictable Plant: An Exploration in Vocational Holiness* (Grand Rapids: Eerdmans, 1992), 192.

Chapter 4 / Buoyed by and Drowned in Community

1. Parker Palmer, *The Promise of Paradox: A Celebration of Contradictions in the Christian Life* (Notre Dame, IN: Ave Maria Press, 1980), 82.

2. Ibid.

Chapter 5 / Breathing in Unison

1. For this idea of recycled and recirculated air I am indebted to Barbara Brown Taylor, "The Gospel of the Holy Spirit" in Barbara Brown Taylor, *Home by Another Way* (Cambridge, MA: Cowley Publications, 1999), 142–43.

2. Dietrich Bonhoeffer, *Life Together: A Discussion of Christian Fellowship* (San Francisco: HarperCollins, 1954), 27.

3. Ibid., 28.

Chapter 6 / The Holy Longing for Connection

1. Ronald Rolheiser, *The Holy Longing: The Search for a Christian Spirituality* (New York: Doubleday, 1999), 22, 28.

2. Ibid., 17.

3. Ibid., 23.

4. Annie Dillard, *Teaching a Stone to Talk: Expeditions and Encounters* (New York: HarperCollins, 1982), 52.

5. Rolheiser, *The Holy Longing*, 25.

6. Anthony de Mello, *Awareness: The Perils and Opportunities of Reality* (New York: Doubleday, 1990), 172.

7. Ibid.

8. Ibid., 174.

9. Ibid., 175.

10. Ibid.

Chapter 7 / Don't You Believe in Love?

1. For the history of the beginnings of courtly love and the romantic ideal in Western literary culture, see Albrecht Classen's *Literary Encyclopedia* article "Courtly Love, *Amour Courtois* (1000–1600)," at *www.litencyc.com*. See also Robert A. Johnson, *We: Understanding the Psychology of Romantic Love* (San Francisco: HarperCollins, 1983).

2. Classen, "Courtly Love."

3. Ibid.

4. Ibid.

5. His Holiness the Dalai Lama and Howard C. Cutler, *The Art of Happiness: A Handbook for Living* (New York: Riverhead Books, 1998), 106.

6. Ibid.

7. Ibid., 107.

8. Sharon Olds, *The Unswept Room* (New York: Alfred A. Knopf, 2003), 7. The poem ends with someone coming to take the infant to the mother.

9. Quoted in *The Art of Happiness*, 111.

10. Thomas Moore, *SoulMates: Honoring the Mysteries of Love and Relationship* (New York: HarperCollins, 1994), 143.

11. Ibid., 144.

12. Eckhart Tolle, *The Power of Now: A Guide to Spiritual Enlightenment* (Novato, CA: New World Library, 1999, 2004), 150.

13. Ibid., 152.

Chapter 8 / The Search for Sexual Fulfillment

1. Lewis B. Smedes, *Sex for Christians* (Grand Rapids: Eerdmans, 1994), 108; quoted in Lauren Winner, *Real Sex: The Naked Truth about Chastity* (Grand Rapids: Brazos Press, 2005), 40.

2. Winner, *Real Sex*, 29–30.

3. Ibid., 38.

4. C. S. Lewis, *The Screwtape Letters* (New York: Simon & Schuster, 1961), 80–81. Lewis might be alluding to a poem in Rilke's *Book of Hours:* "They call 'mine' their walls of stone, / but do not know the Lord of their home. / They say 'mine' and call it theirs although, / everything withdraws when they approach"; see *The Book of Hours: Prayers to a Lowly God,* 159. Regarding religious matters people can be taught, says Lewis, "to reduce all these senses to that of 'my boots,' the 'my' of ownership."

5. Winner, *Real Sex,* 100. See also her chapters on the practices of the viewing of pornography and masturbation (110–17), practices that suggest sex happens outside a relationship.

6. Roland Rolheiser, *Against an Infinite Horizon: The Finger of God in Our Ordinary Lives* (New York: Crossroad, 2001), 65.

7. Ibid., 94–95.

8. Tolle, *The Power of Now,* 150.

Chapter 9 / The Promise and Price of Solitude

1. Roy L. Honeycutt, "Exodus," in *The Broadman Bible Commentary,* vol. 1, rev. ed. (Nashville: Broadman Press, 1973), 297–98.

2. Belden C. Lane, *The Solace of Fierce Landscapes: Exploring Desert and Mountain Spirituality* (New York: Oxford University Press, 1998), 101.

3. Ibid., 114.

Chapter 10 / Solitude as a Christian Lifestyle

1. John D. Barbour, *The Value of Solitude: The Ethics and Spirituality of Aloneness in Autobiography* (Charlottesville: University of Virginia Press, 2004), 12–13.

2. Laura Swan, *The Forgotten Desert Mothers: Sayings, Lives, and Stories of Early Christian Women* (Mahwah, NJ: Paulist Press, 2001), 9.

3. *The Desert Fathers,* trans. Helen Waddell (New York: Sheed and Ward, 1936), 24.

4. Yoshi Nomura, *Desert Wisdom: Sayings from the Desert Fathers,* intro. Henri J. M. Nouwen (New York: Doubleday, 1984), xii.

5. Swan, *The Forgotten Desert Mothers,* 13.

6. *The Life of the Desert Fathers: The Historia Monachorum in Aegypto,* trans. Norman Russell, intro. Benedicta Ward (London: Mowbray, and Kalamazoo: Cistercian Publications, 1981), 27, 105.

7. William Harmless, S.J., *Desert Christians: An Introduction to the Literatures of Early Monasticism* (New York: Oxford University Press, 2004), 327.

8. Ibid., 326–27.

Chapter 11 / The Cost of Discipleship

1. Dietrich Bonhoeffer, *The Cost of Discipleship* (New York: Macmillan, 1963), 105.

2. Ibid., 108–9.

3. Ibid., 110–11.

4. Sandra M. Schneiders, I.H.M., *Selling All: Commitment, Consecrated Celibacy, and Community in Catholic Religious Life* (Mahwah, NJ: Paulist Press, 2001), 227.

5. Ibid., 232.

6. Barbara Brown Taylor, "High-Priced Discipleship," in *Bread of Angels* (Cambridge, MA: Cowley Publications, 1997), 49.

7. Bonhoeffer, *The Cost of Discipleship,* 99.

Chapter 12 / One True Necessity

1. A. Cleveland Coxe, "Introductory Note to the Epistle Concerning the Martyrdom of Polycarp," originally published in 1885; reprinted in *Ante-Nicene Fathers,* vol. 1: *The Apostolic Fathers, Justin Martyr, Irenaeus* (Peabody, MA: Hendrickson Publishers, 1999), 37.

2. From "The Encyclical Epistle of the Church at Smyrna: Concerning the Martyrdom of the Holy Polycarp" in *Ante-Nicene Fathers,* 1:39.

3. Ibid.

4. Based on Polycarp's martyrdom as rendered in "The Encyclical Epistle of the Church at Smyrna," 41; paraphrased.

5. Ibid., 42; paraphrased. The original translation reads: "I give Thee thanks that Thou hast counted me worthy of this day and this hour, that I should have a part in the number of Thy martyrs, in the cup of Thy Christ, to the resurrection of eternal life, both of soul and body, through the incorruption [imparted] by the Holy Ghost."

6. Clement of Alexandria, "The Stromata, or Miscellanies" in *Ante-Nicene Fathers*, vol. 2: *Fathers of the Second Century: Hermas, Tatian, Athenagoras, Theophilus, and Clement of Alexandria*, ed. Alexander Roberts and James Donaldson (Peabody, MA: Hendrickson Publishers, 1999), 411.

7. Ibid., 412.

8. Methodius, "The Banquet of the Ten Virgins," trans. William R. Clark, *Ante-Nicene Fathers*, vol. 6: *Gregory Thaumaturgus, Dionysius the Great, Julius Africanus, Anatolius and Minor Writers, Methodius, Arnobius*, ed. Alexander Roberts and James Donaldson (Peabody, MA: Hendrickson Publishers, 1995), 309–55.

9. For a more detailed discussion of celibacy in the early church, see Annemarie S. Kidder, *Women, Celibacy, and the Church: Toward a Theology of the Single Life* (New York: Crossroad, 2003), esp. 64–103.

10. Peter Brown, *The Body and Society: Men, Women, and Sexual Renunciation in Early Christianity* (New York: Columbia University Press, 1988), 64.

Chapter 13 / Living by the Rule

1. Cyprian, "The Epistles of Cyprian" in *Ante-Nicene Fathers*, vol. 5: *Hippolytus, Cyprian, Caius, Novatian*, ed. Alexander Roberts and James Donaldson (Peabody, MA: Hendrickson, 1999), 367.

2. Most of the information about Benedict, including his twin sister Scholastica—also a monastic, comes from Pope Gregory the Great (590–604), whose purpose in writing the second book of *The Dialogues* was to show that there were holy people not just in the East, but also in Italy.

3. *The Rule of St. Benedict in English*, ed. Timothy Fry, O.S.B. (Collegeville, MN: Liturgical Press, 1982), 18–19.

4. *Catechism of the Catholic Church* (Liguori, MO: Liguori Publications, 1994), no. 915, no. 918.

5. Joan D. Chittister, O.S.B., *Wisdom Distilled from the Daily: Living the Rule of St. Benedict Today* (San Francisco: HarperCollins, 1991), 42–43.

6. Ibid., 156–57.

7. Esther de Waal, *Seeking God: The Way of St. Benedict* (Collegeville, MN: Liturgical Press, 1984), 57.

8. Diogenes Allen, *Temptation* (Cambridge. MA: Cowley Publications, 1986), 88.

9. *The Norton Anthology of Poetry*, rev. shorter ed. (New York: W. W. Norton, 1975), 403.

10. Chittister, *Wisdom Distilled from the Daily*, 9.

Chapter 14 / Starting with the Questions

1. Rainer Maria Rilke, *Briefe an einen jungen Dichter* (Letters to a Young Poet), 3rd Letter (Leipzig: Insel Verlag, 1929), 19; my translation.

2. Ibid., 4th Letter, 23.

3. Ibid., 4th Letter, 26.

4. Ibid., 4th Letter, 26–27.

Chapter 16 / Locking Up the Ego

1. "Privacy, some measure of it, is essential to our souls," Sue Halpern writes in her introduction. "It is essential not only to the souls of painters and poets, who thrive on solitude, but to the rest of us, too— individuals whose canvas is our lives"; in Sue Halpern, *Migrations to Solitude: The Quest for Privacy in a Crowded World* (New York: Random House, 1992), ix.

2. Among these letters are commonly cited Colossians and Philemon, and perhaps Ephesians as well. See Ronald Brownrigg, *Who's Who in The New Testament* (New York: Oxford University Press, 1993), 202.

3. In a letter of May 5, 1943 (mistakenly dated April 5 in the original), to his brother-in-law Hans von Dohnanyi, in Dietrich Bonhoeffer, *Letters and Papers from Prison,* ed. Eberhard Bethge (New York: Simon and Schuster, 1997), 32.

4. Ibid., 33–34.

5. After Bonhoeffer was executed by the Nazis on April 9, 1945, Eberhard Bethge became his biographer. Bethge attended several universities, receiving a doctor of divinity degree, before attending the secret Finkenwalde Seminary, where Bonhoeffer was president and taught the doctrines of Germany's Confessing (anti-Nazi) Church. He became Bonhoeffer's close friend and confidant, and he also married Bonhoeffer's niece, Renate.

6. In a letter dated June 4, 1944. Bonhoeffer, *Letters and Papers from Prison,* 319.

7. Ibid.

8. Enclosed with two other poems, "Christians and Pagans" and "Night Voices in Tegel," in a letter dated July 8, 1944. Ibid., 347–48.

9. Anthony Lee Brown, "A Penitent's Perspective," *Eclectica Magazine,* 1997, at *www.eclectica.org/v1n5/tony.html.*

10. Ibid.

11. Peterson, *Under the Unpredictable Plant,* 90.

Chapter *17* / *Body and Soul on the Treadmill*

1. Lecture by Brian McLaren, "Public Worship as Spiritual Formation," at the conference on Worship, Art, Liturgy, and Preaching in the Emerging Culture (WALP), Asbury Seminary, Wilmore, Kentucky, April 19, 2005.

2. Sunday bulletin from Knox Church — PC (USA) of August 28, 2005.

3. John Wesley, "Upon Our Lord's Sermon on the Mount VI," Sermon 26, based on the 1872 edition; see *www.gbgm-umc.org/UMhistory/ Wesley/sermons/serm-026.stm#mercy.*

4. Ibid.

5. Brian D. McLaren, *A Generous Orthodoxy: Why I Am a Missional and Evangelical and Post/Protestant and Liberal/Conservative and Mystical/Poetic and Biblical and Charismatic/Contemplative and Fundamentalist/Calvinist and Anabaptist/Anglican and Methodist and Catholic and Green and Incarnational and Depressed-Yet-Hopeful and Emergent and Unfinished Christian* (Grand Rapids: Zondervan, 2004), 216.

6. Ibid., 219.

7. Ibid., 220.

8. Margaret Guenther, *Holy Listening: The Art of Spiritual Direction* (Boston: Cowley Publications, 1992), 55.

9. *The Desert Fathers,* trans. Helen Waddell (New York: Sheed and Ward, 1936), 87.

10. Guenther, *Holy Listening,* 55.

11. Peterson, *Under the Unpredictable Plant,* 186–87.

Chapter *18* / *Body Guards*

1. During 2004–5, an average 1.8 million Americans were tuned to one of the four twenty-four-hour channels — CNN, CNBC, Fox, and MSNBC—at any given time, according to Nielsen Media Research; that was up from 920,000 in 1999–2000, a trend similar in prime time. See Bruce Taylor Seeman, "Din of 24-Hour News Is Bad News for Many," *Ann Arbor News,* July 28, 2005, A7.

2. In a confessional style, Donna Marie Williams recounts her growing decision to embrace the celibate lifestyle, at least for a time. "Lord knows I could never be a nun. Although I love the idea of daily communion with the Divine, I absolutely abhor the idea of a lifelong commitment to celibacy. No men? At all? *Ever?* Just the thought makes me want to reach for the Prozac....I love my women friends, but only Man can jump-start my heart and body in that special way that makes the sun shine, the moon glow, and the birds sing their songs"; see Donna

Marie Williams, *Sensual Celibacy: The Sexy Woman's Guide to Using Abstinence for Recharging Your Spirit, Discovering Your Passions, Achieving Greater
Intimacy in Your Next Relationship* (New York: Simon and Schuster, 1999),
12–13.

3. Wendy Keller, *The Cult of the Born-Again Virgin: How Single Women
Can Reclaim Their Sexual Power* (Deerfield Beach, FL: Health Communications, Inc., 1999), xix.

4. Census data can be accessed at *http://factfinder.census.gov.* The
specific data is listed under the topic "marital status."

5. "Book V—On Fornication" in *The Desert Fathers,* 106–7.

6. See *www.halljewelers.com/chastityrings.* Another chastity Web
site, *www.chastitycall.org/ring,* lists viewer questions concerning the ring.
Question: "Where can I order such a ring?" Answer: "I think our gold
chastity rings are $100. The profit from the ring goes to help keep our
shelters open. I personally wear the ring. It is a gold dove. But did you
know you can use any ring as a chastity ring? You could, if you want
to, go to a Christian Store or a jewelry store and purchase something
that has a religious theme for the ring. The idea is to wear it on your
wedding ring finger until it is replaced (maybe) some day by a wedding ring. It can be blessed by a priest or minister and a pledge can be
made before members of your family or friends. The experience could
be simple and private...just between God and you OR more public. And
every single day as you wear the ring, you can be proud to put it on
knowing you have put on a new you and know how truly proud God is
that you have honored Him and His Word with your pledge to be pure in
thought, word and deed. The ring is much more than a piece of jewelry.
It is symbol of your love of God and your commitment to Him to show
your love by honoring His desire for you to be close to Him and His Most
Holy Spirit."

7. The association's Web site is at *www.consecratedvirgins.org.* The
Web site provides a historical overview of the rite of consecrated virginity dating back to the first century and reinstituted in 1970 by the
Roman Catholic Church, following the Second Vatican Council. The Web
site also includes devotional material, contact information, and a statis-
tical overview by geographical region of consecrated virgins worldwide
(with France, Argentina, and Italy showing the highest numbers).

8. Augustine, "Sermons on New Testament Lessons," in *Nicene and
Post-Nicene Fathers,* vol. 6, ed. Philip Schaff, trans. R. G. MacMullen
(Peabody, MA: Hendrickson Publishers, 1995), 402, 405.

Chapter 19 / Charting the Landscape of the Soul

1. John Macquarrie, "Spirit and Spirituality," in *Exploring Christian Spirituality: An Ecumenical Reader,* ed. Kenneth J. Collins (Grand Rapids: Baker Books, 2000), 67.

2. See a 1966 letter to Sufi scholar Abdul Aziz, where Merton gives an account of his hermitage life, and the cycles of prayer, manual labor, and study in Jim Forest, *Living with Wisdom: A Life of Thomas Merton* (Maryknoll, NY: Orbis Books, 1991), 170–71.

3. Thomas Merton, *Thoughts in Solitude* (New York: Farrar, Straus and Giroux, 1956), 47–48.

4. Ibid., 48.

5. Ibid., 48–49.

6. Ibid., 50–51.

7. For the development of Merton's thought on solitude, see Richard Anthony Cashen, *Solitude in the Thought of Thomas Merton* (Kalamazoo, MI: Cistercian Publications, 1981); quoted and summarized in "Thomas Merton on Solitude," an article on the webzine *Hermitary: Resources and Reflections on Hermits and Solitude,* at *www.hermitary.com.*

8. Ibid.

9. Ursula King, *Christian Mystics: Their Lives and Legacies throughout the Ages* (Mahwah, NJ: Paulist Press, 2001), 3–5.

10. Ibid., 229.

11. A proposal for an article, tentatively titled "Speaking Out for the Inside," sent as letter to John Hunt, December 18, 1966; see *Thomas Merton: Essential Writings,* ed. and intro. Christine M. Bochen (Maryknoll, NY: Orbis Books, 2004), 52–53.

12. Thomas Merton, *Contemplation in a World of Action* (New York: Doubleday, 1971), 170; see Merton, *Essential Writings,* 53.

13. Letter to Dom Francis Decroix, August 21, 1967, in *The Hidden Ground of Love: The Letters of Thomas Merton on Religious Experience and Social Concerns,* ed. William H. Shannon (New York: Farrar, Straus and Giroux, 1985), 158; see Merton, *Essential Writings,* 54.

14. Letter to Dom Francis Decroix, August 22, 1967, in *The Hidden Ground of Love,* 159; see Thomas Merton, *Essential Writings,* 54.

15. Thomas Keating, O.S.C.O., *Intimacy With God* (New York: Crossroad, 1994), 42.

16. Eugene H. Peterson, *The Contemplative Pastor: Returning to the Art of Spiritual Direction* (Grand Rapids: William B. Eerdmans, 1989), 84–85.

17. David Steindl-Rast, O.S.B., with Sharon Lebell, *The Music of Silence: Entering the Sacred Space of Monastic Experience* (San Francisco: HarperCollins, 1995), 90.

18. Ibid., 17–18.

19. Pierre Teilhard de Chardin, *Writings, Selected with an Introduction by Ursula King* (Maryknoll, NY: Orbis Books, 1999), 9–10.

20. *The Oxford Book of Prayer,* ed. George Appleton (New York: Oxford University Press, 1985), 352.

21. Elizabeth Roberts, *Earth Prayers from Around the World: 365 Prayers, Poems, and Invocations for Honoring the Earth* (New York: HarperCollins, 1991), 10.

22. *The Oxford Book of Prayer,* 352.

23. Pierre Teilhard de Chardin, "Hymn to Matter" in *Heart of Matter* (New York: Harcourt Brace Jovanovich, 1978), 71–76; see Teilhard de Chardin, *Writings,* 45.

24. "Cosmic Life" in *Writings in Time of War* (New York: Harper & Row, 1968), 60–62; see Teilhard de Chardin, *Writings,* 50.

25. Teilhard de Chardin, *Writings,* 50–51.

26. "My Universe" in *Science and Christ* (New York: Harper & Row, 1968), 44–49, 51; see Teilhard de Chardin, *Writings,* 64–65.

27. *Le Milieu Divin: An Essay on the Interior Life* (New York: Harper & Brothers, 1960), 100–103, 108–9; see Teilhard de Chardin, *Writings,* 73.

28. Teilhard de Chardin, *Writings,* 70–71.

29. "The Mass on the World," in *Heart of Matter* (New York: Harcourt Brace Jovanovich, 1978), 130–34; see Teilhard de Chardin, *Writings,* 109.

30. Teilhard de Chardin, *Writings,* 111.

31. Ibid., 109.

Conclusion

1. Richard Rohr, *Simplicity: The Art of Living,* trans. Peter Heinegg (New York: Crossroad, 1991), 89–90. A newly revised and updated edition of this book is available, *Simplicity: The Freedom of Letting Go* (New York: Crossroad, 2004).

2. Thomas Merton, "Song: If You Seek..." in *The Collected Poems of Thomas Merton* (New York: New Directions, 1977), 340–41; see Thomas Merton, *Essential Writings,* 80. Quoted is the last portion of the poem.

About the Author

Annemarie S. Kidder is associate pastor at the First Presbyterian Church of Ann Arbor, Michigan. She has served as English translator for major German works, including works by Jürgen Becker, Raimon Panikkar, and Luise Schottroff. She is editor and translator of Rainer Maria Rilke's *The Book of Hours: Prayers to a Lowly God* and the Rilke anthology *Pictures of God: Rilke's Religious Poetry.* And she has authored *Women, Celibacy, and the Church: Toward a Theology of the Single Life.*

Kidder holds degrees from the Academy of the Arts in Berlin (M.A.), the School of Journalism at Columbia–Missouri (M.A.), and the Southern Baptist Theological Seminary in Louisville, Kentucky (Ph.D.), in the areas of systematic theology and New Testament literature.

Index

Of Related Interest

Karen Kuchan, Ph.D.
VISIO DIVINA
A New Practice of Prayer
for Healing and Growth

A remarkable new development
in Christian prayer!

Join others today who are finding God's healing, forgiveness, and love through Visio Divina.
In *Visio Divina,* meditative and healing prayer is
used with a particular image that God reveals
for the discovery of hidden wounds and desires.
Dr. Kuchan weaves together practical explanations of this new practice, along with stories of
people who have used it to overcome shame and
anger as they discover divine acceptance and
love.

Karen Kuchan is the founder and president of the
Incarnation Center for Spiritual Growth and an
adjunct professor at Fuller Seminary in Pasadena,
California.

0-8245-2317-2, paperback

crossroad

Of Related Interest

Timothy Gallagher, O.M.V.
THE DISCERNMENT OF SPIRITS
An Ignatian Guide for Everyday Living

By providing a sound understanding of Ignatian principles and applying them in a skillful way to daily life, Father Gallagher meets the pressing needs of retreat directors, retreatants, students of spiritual theology, and others interested in deepening their spiritual lives. I know of no comparable volume that proves so helpful.

—Harvey D. Egan, S.J., Professor of Systematic
and Mystical Theology, Boston College
(from the book's foreword)

Although St. Ignatius of Loyola, founder of the Jesuits, is one of the most influential spiritual leaders of all time, most readers find his Rule hard to understand. Gallagher, an authority and gifted teacher, helps us understand the Rule and how its insights are essential for our spiritual growth today.

0-8245-2291-5, paperback

crossroad

Of Related Interest

Fr. Timothy Gallagher, O.M.V.
THE EXAMEN PRAYER
Ignatian Wisdom for Our Lives Today

With a foreword by Fr. George Aschenbrenner

This is the first book to explain the examen prayer, one of the most popular practices in Christian spirituality. Fr. Timothy Gallagher takes us deep into the prayer, showing that the prayer Ignatius of Loyola believed to be at the center of the spiritual life is just as relevant to our lives today.

Topics include: Desire ~ A Day with Ignatius ~ Gratitude ~ Petition ~ Review ~ Discernment ~ Forgiveness ~ Our Image of God ~ The Future ~ Flexibility ~ The Freedom of the Spirit ~ The Contemplative Capacity ~ Journaling ~ Renewal ~ Courage ~ Spiritual Consolation ~ Letting Go ~ Fruits ~ Discerning Awareness throughout the Day

0-8245-2367-9, paperback

crossroad

Of Related Interest

Timothy Gallagher, O.M.V.
SPIRITUAL CONSOLATION
An Ignatian Guide
for the Greater Discernment of Spirits

"This book presents to committed, busy Christians Ignatius's Second Week Rules for Discernment. Ignatius's teaching here is a treasure that good people desperately need.... Fr. Timothy Gallagher writes exceptionally clearly and attractively about these Second Week Rules. His writing is marked by a reverence and love for Ignatius's text, and by a gift for clear exposition. He charts a wise course through the academic discussions, and his footnotes will provide ample guidance for those who want to explore them further. He shows how real people can be helped by what can sound so arcane when you read Ignatius's text straight off. This book is a valuable new contribution to the Ignatian literature, one that I welcome warmly. Read it and learn from it."

—Philip Endean S.J., Editor, *The Way*

This book is both the completion of Fr. Timothy Gallagher's esteemed Ignatian trilogy and a provocative work in its own right.

0-8245-2429-2, paperback

crossroad

Of Related Interest

Thomas Keating
INTIMACY WITH GOD
An Introduction to Centering Prayer

"For all those aspiring to a genuine spiritual life, Father Keating has charted a course that will take us progressively closer to our divine goal as we learn to touch God, first with the words of our lips, then with reflections of the mind and with the feelings of the heart."   —*Living Prayer*

"Multifarious are the books on prayer and spirituality. Now and then, one sparkles.... This is such a book."   —*Praying*

0-8245-1588-9, paperback

Check your local bookstore for availability.
To order directly from the publisher,
please call 1-800-707-0670 for Customer Service
or visit our Web site at *www.cpcbooks.com.*
For catalog orders, please send your request to the address below.

THE CROSSROAD PUBLISHING COMPANY
16 Penn Plaza, Suite 1550
New York, NY 10001

All prices subject to change.

crossroad